COENRAAD VAN HOUTEN was ........ in the Netherlands
in 1922. After studying Chemistry, ......................
Pedagogy', he lived and worked in Holland, Indonesia, Hong
Kong and Britain as a manager in business, as a consultant,
and as the director of the Centre for Social Development
(which he co-founded). He has developed specialist programmes and seminars for educating adults, and presently
advises organizations on training programmes. He is the
author of *Awakening the Will*, *Practising Destiny*, *The
Threefold Nature of Destiny Learning*, and the co-founder of
the New Adult Learning Movement.

# Creative Spiritual Research

## Awakening the Individual Human Spirit

Coenraad J. van Houten

TEMPLE LODGE

Temple Lodge Publishing
Hillside House, The Square
Forest Row, RH18 5ES

www.templelodge.com

Published by Temple Lodge 2011

A catalogue record for this book is available from the British Library

ISBN 978 1 906999 28 5

Cover by Andrew Morgan Design
Typeset by DP Photosetting, Neath, West Glamorgan
Printed and bound by Gutenberg Press, Malta

MIX
Paper from
responsible sources
FSC
www.fsc.org    FSC® C022612

# Contents

# Acknowledgements

I wish to acknowledge the many colleagues, friends and course participants who provided the working field for this research. Their activity will continue in future, just as this book is to be considered work in progress.

Especially I acknowledge Shirley van Houten who collaborated in the research and in writing down the results for this book. Gratitude goes also to several translators who dealt with differences in English and German languages; particularly I want to mention Norbert Gaertner, Nicole Kringe, Irene Bulasikis, and Sophie Pannitschka.

# Foreword: A Short Account of the Author's Research Process

Coenraad van Houten's journey began with a question: 'How do adults learn and develop?' And also: 'How can adult learning become a living, growing process?'

The questioning began while he was still a youngster, at a Waldorf School where there were teachers who had a new way of thinking. 'I want to do this,' he said to himself. Further education experience took him through academia and 'dead' scientific thinking. Then came wartime and its hard disciplines. After having gained business experience he then did a university training in social pedagogy. The research question began a new life in management consulting with NPI in Holland and global travelling. This led on to an adult education centre in England called 'The Centre for Social Development' where the learning research was further tried and deepened through practice with colleagues and students. Out of his continuing spiritual study of sources behind this field came a new course, the 'Anthroposophical Schooling Course'.

In this schooling course, held at the Centre for Social Development from the beginning of 1989, the learning process was researched and deepened further through practice, always by observation of processes and results. The original research question burned on in him through all the years, with variations and specific aspects to be developed. Typical of research processes is that because you have the question you are alert to what speaks to it, or to new insights including those of helpers. This was a very rich gathering process over years, from many sources. Coenraad's whole biography can be seen as contributing to the basic research question that has been his life mission. Now at 88 years he wanted to write down the research results to date. The research, however, is never finished, each result leading to another step or another question.

One landmark on the way was finding in Rudolf Steiner's book *The Riddle˙ of Humanity* an indication about the 12 senses and the seven life processes of the human constitution. Steiner simply indicated them with little explanation. The seven life or 'etheric' processes maintain our bodily existence, but they are also forces we can use in adult life for learning and spiritual enlightenment. This was an 'Aha' moment in his research—'Here is an important indication; it is *obvious* this is the material to work with.' After the 'Aha' intuition moment came the difficult process of working it out in practice. The result of this process can be found in the author's first book, *Awakening the Will*—written for educators to present a 'living learning for adults' (published 1993). See also p. 24.

Then came another 'helper'—a friend who had read this and said, 'But could this not also apply to learning from life or destiny? Maybe it would look like this...' Reading the letter Coenraad had the immediate intuition 'yes, but this is not correct'. So began the next phase of research, into learning from destiny. He used his own instrument, his own learning from destiny, as part of the material for the research. He used observation of human phenomena, what happens to people and how they deal with it. His spiritual background was an essential source of how to look and how to question the phenomena. The result of this research process you can read in the author's second book, *Practising Destiny* (published 1998). Further development of this learning led to a third book, *The Threefold Nature of Destiny Learning* (published 2003), where exercises discovered through practice are offered to complete the application of the seven life processes to this learning path.

But another question remained ... there must be a third learning path. It is inherent in the human being that we develop in a threefold way. He pondered long—it must have something to do with the inner spiritual path of the individual. Out of the background of the esoteric school of Rudolf Steiner, it became clear: it is the path of spiritual research and human creativity. Research into this was quite another process, since it involves thresholds of consciousness and the inner schooling of the individual. The creative insights come from spiritual sources, prepared in our earthly awareness, and understood and carried out in earthly application—three steps up, the 'Aha', and three steps down. This path of research touched every level of his own inner path, meeting crises, difficulties, new faculties to be prepared, encounters, thresholds, and what Steiner called the Guardian of the Threshold. Experience proved that the three steps down, to incarnate the new discovery, are the most difficult. Exploring this learning path began in the schooling course in 1994 and continues by practising with and through colleagues who share this research process.

These three learning paths, based on the seven life processes as medium, are the basic work of the NALM—New Adult Learning Movement. The NALM is the final initiative of C. van Houten to bring his research into the adult learning field.

The research that brought about this book is in itself an example of the creative spiritual research learning path:

1. The question that destiny awakened and then led his life and inner journey.
2. The ever-continuing presence of the question, motivating his search, using himself as instrument.
3. Personal life experiences and destiny as research material, with miraculous help from many sources; both outward and inward exploration.
4. Moments of insight, the exceptional state or breakthrough of something new.
5. Condensing the insight into an understandable form for others. What does it really mean?
6. Testing the discovery in practice, for contemporary needs.
7. Presenting it in courses and seminars. Then writing it down in a book—and giving it away for others to take further.

Many people, in different parts of the world, who worked with the material have been a strong support in this final part of the spiritual research path of learning. The final three processes, 5, 6 and 7, were only possible with the involvement of many colleagues.

*Shirley van Houten*

Shirley van Houten, who has been a colleague in this work since 1989, assisted with writing down the results of Coenraad's research for this book.

# Introduction

## Our global context

The world has changed and is going through tremendous upheavals in its change process. The human constitution has also changed and is going through similar inner upheavals.

A spiritual paradigm shift is evident. In spite of extremely difficult circumstances, one must go ahead nevertheless in creating our future human conditions.

It is no longer enough to study and understand spiritual matters. Now it must be *done*—'for yourself in the situation where you are'. This requires a further step from basic inner schooling to awaken the inner creative spirit which is slumbering within the human being. The potential is there to be a creative being. Human creativity is the basis for the future. The consequences of what people are doing now will in the larger sense create a new human culture.

It is necessary and urgent to take steps in this direction. This is part of the paradigm shift of consciousness—that we are taking on the future of the planet and of mankind. This position has never existed before in our evolution.

## The individual context

The question now is not so much what we do but *how* to act. Do our deeds do damage or bring sustainable life?

Every grown-up youth has unexpected thoughts or impulses which one does not understand, but which must be pursued somehow. There is arising into awareness the germ of new creative convictions, which show they have future in them.

Almost everyone today comes to deep questions of life— what does it mean, what is real, who am I, what can I do in the world, where are we going, why is it so, what moral values are behind the scene, what is at this moment possible? Etc. etc. Most of these questions will not be satisfied with answers off the Internet. The question leads to a life quest, a research path, ending finally in real deeds.

## The aim of this book

This book wants to support this global and individual spiritual paradigm shift. It will appeal to those who are in touch with their inner creative impulses, or are motivated for it but do not know how to begin. The aim is to make this spiritual path possible for every person. It can change the way one relates to life and work—at first simply by an attitude shift, as a questioning, caring human being, taking seriously the spiritual forces that manifest in all outer phenomena.

In Part One there are guidelines and exercises for individual practice, how to go on a research-learning path through the individualized spirit. For spiritual research the human being itself is the instrument. Therefore research-learning is an inner schooling way that at the same time brings together earthly and spiritual realms. The aim is to be able to work with this immediately, so one can find creative answers to the world we face as soon as possible.

Part Two is about the general schooling path, as preparation or precondition, opening the inner space needed for research and a questioning attitude.

The book is itself the result of spiritual research processes, and should be seen as work in progress. The research will be continuous, always new, but it is important to share what has been found so far.

Out of the understanding that what has to be found is a constant renewal in a continually changing world situation, it became obvious that not only an enquiring mind but also creative social and artistic faculties and finally moral faculties had to be found, as a synthesis of all three. This synthesis may become a new quintessential force in the human being.

## New Adult Learning impulse

The New Adult Learning impulse takes its spiritual sources from indications by Rudolf Steiner, worked through, experienced, and brought into practical application and further development. The intent is for spirituality to become part of everyday life and the modern paradigm shift of consciousness in our time. Therefore the indications of Rudolf Steiner are not quoted or specifically referred to. We can also consider that if he were addressing the conditions of the twenty-first century his spiritual insights would be presented in quite new ways. The consequences of his life and work are available for all to find and are not exclusive.

The greatest difficulty in writing is to show a way towards this spiritual research, in a language that expresses a reality that lives beyond words. What is after all 'spiritual'?

Each person must resolve this according to their own karma and spiritual path—there is no intention to give rules to live by.

As a motif for this work, we may quote words from Rudolf Steiner, at the end of his life:

I yearn to ignite every person
Out of the Cosmic Spirit
That he may become a Flame
And fiery, unfold his being's Being.

The others they would take
From the Cosmic Water
That which extinguishes the flame
And lames all inward being.

O Joy when the human flame
Glows, even then when it rests.

O bitterness, when the human thing
Is bound, there where it wants to be active.

From Rudolf Steiner's notebook at the time of his illness
in 1925

## Why should everyone learn creative spiritual research?

Putting this question rests on the assumption that this is possible, still more that in every human being a more or less concealed spiritual source is present which can be awakened. Appearances seem to contradict this assumption. Many people do not seem to be very creative, do not have any true inner questions, are promptly satisfied with every sort of information, do not have an analysing nature, are often active physically but mentally passive, etc. Another experience shows that among many people, this spiritual source is blocked through all kinds of influences, conceptions and learning methods which result in a conditioning, preventing the slumbering creative spirit to develop. We are unfortunately overfed with information; we live in an 'answer culture', not in a questioning, actively searching culture.

Our starting point is all the questions which one encounters in life and at work and which are not answered in a satisfactory manner through plain information. The spiritually lazy, lethargic human being stops there. The spirited researcher, however, begins there—investigating cognitively, artistically, actively.

Three blockages are mentioned here which can hinder or restrain us to become a researcher:

1. Expanding on the concept of 'creative spiritual research', we do not only mean the researcher who must verify some prior discovery or scientific premiss through strict methods. Many education models demand of the student that everything that has been taught should be exactly repeated. Therefore, from the beginning one does not learn to investigate new matters but only to reproduce what has been described.
2. The so-called 'professional deformation' can have a powerful effect. After 10–15 years on the job, whatever his vocation, a person often becomes fixed in his attitude and ways and so does not carry out a continuous development

process. Often one can determine by someone's outer behaviour whether he is a salesman, civil servant, actor, advocate, policeman or departmental manager. The individual gets used to following a certain logic, which has in one field a certain legitimacy, but which is not valid in other fields. 3. The powerful structure in organizations that are over-controlled or hierarchical leads to the conditioning of the people who work in them, and limit their creativity. The same can go for other work organizations with their specializations and their specific culture.

If we really look at our world, we encounter innumerable riddles, not only in the observation of nature but also in reflecting on culture. Because of political and economic media techniques, which become ever more technically sophisticated, if we are not to become helpless victims unconsciously conditioned and manipulated we must pay heed with an increased consciousness and discernment to come to an independent, sensible judgement.

Thus learning through spiritual research is a necessity for survival because each thought, responsibility and creative activity is in danger of succumbing to illusions or creating a virtual-reality world. Thus creative form of learning must be the main aim of all present-day adult education and everything that has been previously described is a learning path to reach this aim.

Indeed, if our present assumption is true that everyone has a predisposition to creativity, then on the whole human beings are in a condition of 'sleep' nowadays and therefore below their spiritual potential. This is not only a 'waste' but also points to something unhealthy in our culture, leading even to personal impairment.

In a few words one can mention therefore some reasons why learning through creative spiritual research is important for us:

1. In order to be able in one's work to explore questions for which there seems to be no solution, and to find new answers.
2. To be able to overcome vocational numbness and defor-

mation. In every vocation new conditions and developments
accelerate so that new faculties must be continuously worked
out, while old ones have to be amplified or changed.
3. A fundamentally questioning, researching, investigating
attitude belongs to the spiritual health of mankind. It nourishes the spirit of man. It changes the viewpoint on life
situations, and can reveal a new meaning.
4. All progress in our time has been founded on research. Our
culture is not imaginable without research. Therefore it follows that a basic attitude of creative researching should be
cultivated in all education work, so that we could be schooled
to become modern up-to-date beings.
5. The past can be released and creative action found in the
present moment, in the reality of the present situation and its
future potential.
6. Very important is realizing one's basic life task, bringing
order into destiny and rediscovering purpose in work. This is
a call to the initiative force of people. This force always
aspires to a creative research attitude in order to progress.

Thus perhaps the most important component is the human
being himself. The more one tries to understand this creature,
one discovers that he is predisposed to, has a longing for, and
bears deep in himself the will, the aspiration, to be a creative
being. The brilliant spirit of Friedrich Schiller already
regarded this as a 'drive to play' in us. Others experience this
as the meaning of their life.

When this 'meaning', due to various life circumstances,
remains undeveloped or blocked, or is even prevented
through many cultural conditionings and other factors, the
creative spirit is dead in that person. It is very distressing to
experience that this is more or less the case for so many
people. Their life feels empty, meaningless, going through a
black hole, or other descriptions of a threshold of self-
confrontation.

Therefore the highest goal of the educator is creative
spiritual research for everybody; yes, culturally considered it
is his other highest duty. In a deep way, to put this into

practice is essential for our spirit and soul health, to work effectively and to heal the impairments of our culture.

## Scientific research and spiritual research

The field of research is huge and expanding, with new discoveries breaking through traditional boundaries of investigation to unknown realms and forces, even to the extent of looking to the Big Bang to see if this supplies on explanation of our creation in the first place. Our theme here addresses the question of what is the difference between 'scientific' and 'spiritual' research?

The scientific disciplines developed in modern times are meant to give a certainty to new discoveries. Spiritual science asks for the same honest discipline in research methods, but explores the invisible reality behind the material world. In this book the term 'spiritual' means those forces, powers, beings, the existence of which the material world is but an outer manifestation or phenomenological expression. The laws of the spiritual realms, however, are quite different from the laws and logic of the physical material realm. Therefore when the forces behind the outer manifestation are understood, the physical world will have another meaning, another kind of solution or answer to our searching questions.

Research is motivated by needs in the world, often driven by business interests for the sake of money and profit, or other kinds of immediate need. Very often the results are quickly applied without an understanding of the forces inherent in them. There are consequences however beyond the immediate pragmatic solutions. The word 'sustainable' has recently appeared in popular vocabulary, in connection with caring for the future of our environment and humanity. It is important to work in harmony with the creative spiritual powers of the universe—which are more intelligent than we human beings will ever be. This harmony will have promise for the future, whereas inventions that counter the benefit of the earth will eventually fall away, and have no future. Thus a healthy attitude to begin any line of research would be respect and wonder for the phenomenon and what it could reveal of its truth.

The research approach herein described is strongly related to the scientific work of Johann Wolfgang von Goethe who penetrated the phenomena, uniting himself with it until the invisible reality spoke to him. He worked mainly in the realm of nature. Rudolf Steiner expanded further on this, connecting to modern consciousness and scientific discipline in nearly every applied field. He was called by Canon Shepherd 'the scientist of the invisible'.

Herein are indicated some similarities and differences of scientific and spiritual research.

Scientific research, as it has been practised in recent centuries, has brought a new basic attitude towards the material world. Old revelation knowledge, traditions, religious faiths and other knowledge authorities were thoroughly left out of consideration. Everything was established on facts, experiments, measurable data, etc. which could undergo observation. Phenomena were explained through theories that are acceptable to reason and that always maintained a provisional hypothesis character, because new perceptions, experiences or facts could contradict them and demand new explanations. Thus a scientific field arose that presented itself as being unstable and demanding inconsistent breakthroughs which overthrew a generally established theory (a new paradigm), with the result that new basic conceptions became necessary. Scientific research shows revolutionary character and produces new paradigms all the time.

The new paradigms come out of intuitive sources, in this manner coming already in the immediate neighbourhood of spiritual research which begins directly with the activity of the human spirit itself as a legitimate path to knowledge. The path of spiritual-scientific knowledge could well present itself as a new paradigm. It offers our modern science a revolutionary jump in which knowledge does not stop at theories that explain phenomena of the world provisionally, but comes to the perception leading to the spiritual essence pervading world phenomena.

Returning to the question of what are the similarities between spiritual research and scientific research and what are the differences, the similarities will be first described:

1. Scientific research demands that statements which are made should be described in a clear language—so that it is communicable and accessible to healthy, logical thinking.
2. Discoveries should be able to be reproduced by others so that they can be investigated.
3. Usually the results are then controlled under existing scientific criteria. This is a tricky situation since the new paradigms are mostly discovered through new methods, and the method controversy often takes the form of vehement resistance against a new conception.

Spiritual research has these three similar criteria of scientific work except, as we shall see, it deals with the method question in a different way; in spite of this the methods applied must be formulated in a precise manner.

The still more fundamental similarity presents itself in the basic attitude of the researcher himself. When a young man the author attended many lectures on psychology, but he was deeply disappointed over the content of the lectures since he was unable to discover anything about the essence of the human soul. However, he had to admire the attitude of the lecturers towards their research work. It was a con-scientiousness, the inner rigour of consequent thinking, never accepting *nor rejecting* something which has not been verified. To examine everything, check, and demand alternative explanations—this demonstrated a new strict sense of truth. Spiritual-scientific research demands in the same way this basic attitude towards research. The continuous maintenance of the sense of truth takes a central position in this book, but this sense of truth has become more and more endangered through outer and inner influences. A heightened sense of truth as a fundamental attitude towards all perceptions is required by scientific research as well as by spiritual research. The ability to distinguish becomes ever more essential, to *know* where you are, what is what, and where does it belong.

This basic scientific attitude is not generally an achievement of our time. Therefore it should be maintained in every education course, so that it can be extended to spiritual research and be applied in daily life each time spiritual questions demand it from us when we encounter them.

So far a few similarities have been outlined, so now let us look at the differences between spiritual research and scientific research:

1. Spiritual research begins with all questions which face us in the encounter with the world, and to which science gives us either no answer or insufficient and unsatisfactory information. For example, science defined water as $H_2O$ but with this definition we obtain no explanation about the essence of water, its significance in nature phenomena, its function in the universe, its origin, its qualities or its existence. Science stops in front of all existential questions and does not consider this as its task. Philosophy and theology could be an exception. But both also stop short of specific questions. Science can give us a lot of information about a certain person, but no answer to his uniqueness, his individuality, because this is not something general and uniqueness does not let itself be quantified through statistics. Finding a spiritual research question will be treated with still more details further below, since all research arises out of the questions which exist within us, and they have different characters in scientific and in spiritual research.

2. The aims of these two forms of research are thus different. The first one leads to a scientific theory which will be provisionally assumed as an explanation, and the other one—spiritual research—leads to a spiritual identity which bears an answer in itself. Thus science leads to a limit which spiritual science wants to overcome. Therefore, spiritual science can be called a broader science, but only if it remains true towards the three scientific criteria mentioned above and bears in itself the modern, conscientious, disciplined fundamental attitude. Spiritual science transgresses the above threshold in front of which science stops.

A true spiritual intuition is also a threshold crossing and in this sense scientific research and spiritual research could work hand in hand. The day could come when spiritual research as a paradigm could be recognized by normal science.

For our education question, it is a fact that we are confronted with so many spiritual questions in our daily life that the schooling of the fundamental attitude and the learning path of spiritual research is unavoidable.

3. A third and crucial difference is that the human being himself is the research instrument in dealing with spiritual questions. In terms of research procedure, this means that new spiritual faculties have to be schooled so that the spiritual essence can be first recognized. This form of learning is dependent on the question process itself and is different according to the many professional fields and sciences. For instance, biological, economical, mathematical , psychological and medical questions need different spiritual faculties for their research path.

4. In two respects this means also a different behaviour towards the pursued methods. In the first place the method becomes at the same time a schooling path. In spiritual science the method is also an inner path, a way to go. Secondly, the method arises out of the question itself and according to the 'spiritual being' who from the other world should and wants to show what we are looking for. Anyone who expects that the spiritual world should obey the method determined by us is not going to get very far. The arrogance that the world must conform to my models and methods has to be overcome. It is necessary, however, that we must later describe exactly which way we followed in order to achieve the research result, so that it can be understood and applied.

As already mentioned, research learning on the spiritual level follows also the seven life processes, but they now become transformed through the fundamental attitude to research. An enhancement takes place which must lead to seven creative research capacities.

In conclusion, it is imperative that each person takes on a

creative researching attitude, in small ways in daily deeds, in work and in relationships, in whatever way is at present possible. There is a fierce battle going on in the world for what kind of forces and life quality we will sustain. The speed of change puts pressure on the researcher to produce results and apply them quickly, without taking the time and deeper research to be aware what kind of forces are being unleashed. On the one hand, without deeper knowledge of the forces that research is gaining access to, our very life is endangered. On the other hand, lack of education for creativity limits human possibility. The future depends on our human activities—co-creating a life that is spirit filled, meaningful and sustainable.

# Part One:
# The Creative Spiritual Learning Path

# 1. What is Creativity and How Does it Arise?

One of the deepest riddles of adult education science is: How can a creature such as the human being create something really new, which did not exist before? The creature becomes creator—that is the highest learning aim! The word 'creativity' indicates that something new *can* be created. New inventions, new ideas, new conceptions, new artistic achievements, new cultures, etc. do come into existence. The human creature is endowed in general with the innate capacity of developing a creative spirit. It is a natural drive in us to want to be creative.

What then is 'creativity'? At best we can express creativity as a *force* in the human being, a natural drive and potential faculty in every person. Promoting this force in all learning is central. A further dimension comes into learning on this, the third, learning path and must be emphasized here: the human being is able to possess and develop a creative spirit.

Creativity will be unique to the individual because of who he is and what background of experiences, development and capacities lives in him. The individual will be able to find new answers and discoveries out of himself, without an inter-mediating initiate, guru, medium or other authority. But this potential can be realized only when one is active to develop it and has refined oneself as a suitable instrument for it. For spiritual research, the human being himself is the instrument.

The assumption here is that true creativity will include connecting with inspiration from spiritual sources, the human placing himself between earthly and spiritual realms and bringing these two realities together. While creativity applies on many levels and in many fields of activity, the highest form in this sense is to freely act out of a new relationship to spiritual worlds, connecting with the cosmic order out of a new way of knowing. In our present state of physical density, the spiritual connecting may be only 'breakthrough' moments; but such moments can last a lifetime in their effect. The 'breakthrough' phenomenon of a new discovery can be described in many ways. However, something new will be apparent each time, whether in the mind, in artistic creativity, in feeling life, in social life, or in moral convictions that are fundamentally new. Man's spirit has a creative predisposition, which can manifest itself in many different ways and on different levels. Joseph Beuys, the artist, referred to creativity as coming out of resurrection forces—out of 'nothing', lifting oneself by one's own forces to a new breakthrough or a new level of awareness. Every real artist knows such moments in an artistic creative process.

Clearly from the perspective here presented, creativity means not only reproducing physically but producing out of spiritual activity, crossing a threshold to another source of reality and bringing this into connection to earthly existence. This is why creativity is related to a spiritual research path. Every initiative needs to be prepared by research to ensure its spiritual validity.

The modern mystery path goes via our will, our deeds, our initiatives, thus our creative activity. The workplace is also an initiation centre if we bring this consciousness to it. Deeds of will come out of a drive to be creative, to act freely in the situation out of creative intuition, free of past convictions or conditioning. To be effective however requires that we *know* in our heart and mind what is the reality of the situation, what forces are involved here, and what consequences may ensue. Spiritual research engenders a new way of knowing. Thus moral will on the one hand and the knowing capacity on the other constitute a polarity between which we find the love force as a selfless objective guide and quality which permeates our actions. This composition of the human being will shine through in a new creative humanness.

*A further word about knowing:* This should not be considered only as a faculty of mind or ability to accumulate knowledge, but also as a deeper sense of reality which can be cognitive knowing, or heart knowing, or intuitive knowing, or better still all three together. It is a faculty hardly explainable in words, but when you have it you know what it is!

The preparation necessary for this can be developed in the first two learning paths as described by the author in earlier books. These two paths had the aims of individualizing all learning and learning from destiny for self-understanding. The creative spiritual research learning path becomes the culmination and purpose of adult learning and self-development. Becoming a creative spiritual researcher can be taught and can be learned.

The learning paths work with the seven life processes of the human life (etheric) organism, seven forces that are available to adults for their learning process. The seventh life process is *reproduction*. For the learning paths this has been identified as *creativity*. Thus we could say that in so far as the ego is active in the process creativity can permeate all learning processes and is the aim and end result. But on what level and in what way is one being 'creative'? What is 'reproduction' as a life process?

Returning to the question as to what is creativity, three archetypal areas could be named:

- the first: bodily reproduction
- the second: social creativity through language, communication, encountering, artistic processes, working together
- the third: spiritual creativity within spiritual research, awakening the individual sense of truth and intuition, to connect earthly deeds and spiritual insight

The first of these, human reproduction, is a natural phenomenon. Children are born out of an encounter between man and woman, but the creation is more than just physical. The child can become an individual human being, transcending its inheritance, with its own destiny and continuity. The love force which brings men and women together is a factor in this creative encounter, as well as the masculine and feminine organism. The human spirit is more than the differences of gender.

A true human encounter is a second example. This really takes place when the two persons involved experience through it a change within themselves. Thus they have received something new. The essential element takes place in the human soul. Language is the mediator in this encounter process.

What is therefore the second archetype of creativity? It is *language,* creation of words. Consonants and vowels encounter each other and create something new in which something essential can create itself. What lives beyond words is made manifest.

Using language becomes an act of conception. Another 'speaking' being hears it, receives it in himself and bears it in his soul where it can ripen.

The receiving, cultivating and letting it grow inwardly is the second phase of the creative process. When it is ripe, it can be born. When this new 'creature' is born it finds a frame on earth in language. Using language and hearing becomes the second creativity ideal in the communion among human beings.

A profound encounter experience can take place when the language spoken carries a karma dimension, spoken out of listening through the words to the destiny forces working between people. This faculty can be spontaneously awakened or can be schooled as a new sense for karma. In future it will become a new social force.

What is now the third ideal of creativity? It appears in our spiritual creativity. It begins in the question. The individual encounters the world and is *spiritually enriched.* The penetration happens through the warming life processes and into inner growth, up to ripening. The 'new' is *born* on earth out of the *spiritual activity.* A new birth takes place.

Creativity is perhaps the deepest mystery, which as a conscious process will include *creative spiritual research itself.* It can be seen as a precondition for a new morality, a new objective love force for humanity, the beginning of a consequence-thinking and conscience for the future.

*A further word about conscience:* What we usually consider

as moral can be an educated set of values we live by, social or spiritual, in the culture of the time and place of our childhood and development and work ethics. Through awakening of consciousness, we start to question this set of values. Does it really belong to my own being, to who I am and my life intentions? An inner voice begins to sound for what is morally right or true. For instance, must I follow the system? Or join the lie to keep my job?

This individual inner voice first speaks for my own soul, then for an inner awareness of situations and what is right for this moment in time and place (not led by a set of laws or principles). A third awakening of the conscience voice connects to spiritual intentions for humanity in its development: the stream of time from the future, towards the ideal human image and a sustainable world future. This level is a first experience of unity between earthly and cosmic forces. The future sustaining of earth and human being will depend on each individual awakening to the capacity for knowing and the inner voice of conscience. It also must become a community force, when people gather around a shared aim with meaning and renewal of life.

On all levels conscience can be experienced as a force towards the future, in how to act in the present moment. All our acts will be consequential; what we do, or do not do, creates the future global condition. It is again an intuitive kind of force in us, not easily explainable but when you have heard the voice of conscience you know what it is.

Creativity will be a situational process at every step, differently oriented if inventing a new product or exercise, or seeking the right karmic deed, or a new spiritual opening. The spiritual research process as it comes to existence can be described in seven steps, relating to the seven life processes. In this way creativity as a faculty becomes learnable.

## Resistances to creativity

This potential to be a creator has not always existed for every human being. We generally considered it the province of special genius or initiates. Because it is a new development, there is of course some ground for resistance, and an accompanying fear of the unknown.

One specific resistance against the creativity concept must be mentioned here. It has its root partly in classical natural science which presumes that relationships are determined purely by cause and effect. Out of such thinking it is difficult to imagine that something truly new can arise out of any form of encounter: coincidence can at most bring something apparently new. Psychology today is still hindered by analytical and causal thinking.

Another source of resistance comes from 'duality' thinking. The many opposite concepts such as friend/enemy, love/hate, good/bad, black/white, man/woman, for/against conceived as causalities forbid the admission of a 'middle' space out of which something new could arise. The computer technology with its yes/no limitation is contributing to this duality thinking. Human creativity occurs out of the centre of the human being which is called 'soul' and which always aims at a balance between many antitheses, such as inner world/outer world, day/night, life/death, thinking/action, nerve-sense system/metabolic-limb system, and many others. Polarities, however, have a middle field, dualities only a relationship depending on causalities. *The birthplace of all creativity lies in the human soul in the 'middle' field, and it begins when a new real question is born in us.*

Transforming the seven life processes to seven research *faculties* is described in the learning path in the following chapters.

## Creativity in three learning paths

### Individualized learning
The first learning path is called 'Awakening the Will'. The aim here is to awaken the individual to his or her own inner spirit centre, igniting a new kind of will force and an independent sense of truth. One learns how to be independent and responsible for all learning, and to digest and absorb learning

on all levels so that knowledge becomes inner capacities and attitudes—something you can creatively work with in life situations. The balanced ego-centred person learns to observe, to see and to assess outer and inner worlds objectively. These observing, questioning faculties will be necessary to stay upright and conscious as a spiritual researcher. They are also necessary faculties for successfully dealing with daily life and work. Rather than being a victim or someone who merely reacts to life, an attitude shift takes place, activating the ego to learn from experiences.

As a result, a creative attitude towards the world is brought about and an awareness of a creative source within oneself. 'Reproduction' as a life process is not 'repeating the same', or regurgitating knowledge, but an original achievement out of one's own creative forces.

**Destiny learning**
The second learning path, which is learning from life and destiny, has another quality and level of creativity. This form of learning is a self-transformation process, going through three stages: recognition and understanding of my destiny; then transforming the resistances and consequences of the past to new capacities; and then becoming creative in taking on my life. An open space is created in which alternative deeds, or behaviour, become possible. In other words, we are able to act freely and creatively in the destiny situations life presents to us. Questions to my own experiences, such as 'why did it happen to me?' and 'how did it speak to my inner world?', may result in a new meaning and direction for life.

It will be very individual what kind of research questions will be presented and what capacities our karmic constitution will allow us to take on in this life. Our task in life and development has also karmic roots from before birth, seen at the 'midnight hour' between lives when we could see the far past and far future. Here in this incarnation each person will have certain creative possibilities and intentions. For instance four possible ways may be:

1.  Bringing order into disorder of karma out of the past, so as to be able to integrate my destiny with the divine world order. Ordering the past may mean to balance one-sided development, make good, bring harmony, etc.
2.  The social art: to see karma as past and future, our acts as consequential for others, and acting in a fruitful way for the social future.
3.  Acts as healing deeds: to bring new qualities into the world out of free will, meaningful within cosmic purpose. The future depends on our deeds. In this sense healing is 'placing oneself correctly into the cosmic order' (Keirle).
4.  A new conscience: vision with regards to the future, as a karmic preview, and consequential awareness.

An important faculty growing in this learning path is the sense of karma, which is a feeling-knowing faculty to be aware of the time stream of life: what belongs to the past and what is streaming towards us from the future. We learn to trust the wisdom in our destiny and the spiritual powers that support our journey. The transformation processes of this destiny learning path are effective in our personal development, in our relationships with others, and in applying our creative forces and new spirit will forces in the practice of life. A new kind of creativity in social life will be the result.

### Creative spiritual research learning
The third learning path is that of learning for spiritual research, which becomes the culmination and purpose of adult learning and inner development. Becoming a spiritual researcher can be taught and can be learned. Being a researcher becomes an attitude and a way of life—maturing from someone who only reacts or is a victim to being a learner, a researcher.

As a researcher it is essential to know oneself and be able to distinguish what is self and otherness when crossing thresholds of consciousness. Soul forces are to be ever more refined so that—for instance—

• thinking has a discerning objectivity and understanding

- feelings can sense the otherness, be one with it selflessly
- willing has an intuitive knowing for the kind of being or reality that is experienced, and a moral motivation for why one is doing the research in the first place.

Therefore an essential new dimension is added to the creativity forces, that of the moral motivation for the research question and the outcome: *'What for?' and 'For what?'* Will the result explode the universe? Will the result build a better future?

Science has been so successful in discovering deep powerful forces, for good or evil use. Will anyone really *use* the nuclear bombs? Creativity is now an existential issue. This applies not only for macro-social issues but also for micro-social needs. How deep is our understanding of the needs and their real solution? Our deeds will be consequential, building earthly and spiritual substance which will determine the life conditions of this planet in the future. It seems nature is adapting to our human activity. Thus creativity must be related to a spiritual research path, to know what forces we are working with.

In the third learning path, our intention shifts from occupation with self-development to the needs of the world. It is fundamental in human nature to be active and to want to contribute, to be able to devote oneself to something. But one cannot give out of nothing—we must first be strong as an individual spirit, then we are able to sacrifice or become one with another without losing our own being. We need to build up our 'spiritual capital'. This learning path is thus creative for an outer purpose, but at the same time creative in development of inner research faculties. Especially important for encountering thresholds of consciousness, for moving between earthly and spiritual worlds, is the schooling of feelings as an organ of perception and inner uprightness.

## 2. Introduction to Creative Spiritual Research as an Individual Learning Path

Learning to do spiritual creative research is the crown of the three learning paths, because without true creativity all methods will become sclerotic ways of work, *useable methodology*, all concepts become dogmas, all processes and attitudes become behaviour patterns.

Today we recognize the problems in society but not the forces behind them, nor do we know how they can be resolved. There is a journey to go from what we see to what we need to do.

Some questions open doors, others close them. The question we see before us and the inner attitude we are radiating carry us to our threshold point. Sometimes it is difficult to find a real question, what the world is asking of us. The important thing is to expand and deepen our capacity for *interest*. Interest awakens the powers of love. Interest keeps you lively, enlivens your etheric body—so you can stay active until 101 years of age! The question becomes a life quest and can lead your spiritual path.

The spiritual is always present within the sense world and is flowing through our sensing activity—only we are limited in our consciousness. All our senses can be enhanced by our activity, by schooling ourselves to become more transparent. How much we are allowed to perceive depends on the inner attitude with which we approach the world. Therefore the schooling of observation is a major part of the work in adult learning to become spiritually active and available to spiritual insights. The ego holds its uprightness, in balance, with just enough outward activity and attentiveness inwardly so the 'new' can appear in between.

The second learning path of destiny learning culminates in an inner attitude change, an *objective love force* for humanity and the world. The third learning path now applies this inner

attitude and love quality in deeds for life, out of inner freedom and choice of motivation. The path has archetypal
processes in research using the seven life processes; but just as
essential are the faculties developed and the changes of consciousness required to bring a new level of understanding to
our deeds.

The learning path for spiritual research requires the
widening, deepening, even transforming to a higher level of
the seven life processes.

For research, there is always the concern how to validate
what we find. Can we judge this out of our own efforts? The
modern way is very individual, but a wise person will seek
companions to confirm findings, and will test out the results
in practice, as will be described in steps 5 and 6, bringing the
research downwards. Most important is to retain a
researcher's attitude at every step, while it happens. Our own
experiences are also to be observed with both attentiveness
and a researcher's outlook. This is a protection and prevents
fantasies or 'flying out'. The researcher goes through
thresholds without losing sense perceptions, stays observing,
stays present, encountering spiritual sources without losing
consciousness.

The path upwards to read the signs and the path downwards to realize what you have discovered spiritually can only
be realized when accompanied with reading your destiny and
developing destiny transformed faculties to be able to act out
of your destiny. Bringing the discovery down is the most
difficult part. Flashes of insight are not unusual today. In
fact, every new generation seems to be born with an increased
consciousness and inborn faculties of perception.

It may be important here to give a few indications with
regard to the schooling of such faculties.

In learning path 1—independent learning—the accent was
on the three ego activities in observation: attentiveness,
devotion and uprightness. These three were supported
through many specific exercises. The importance of these
three faculties does not diminish on this third learning path;
however, they must be schooled to a higher level.

For example, in step 1, in order to be able to become aware of latent phenomena and facts, we need an increased selfless attentiveness. It is the only way of discovering and also understanding the invisible questions which are concealed behind the appearances. We learn to read phenomena in a new way. In step 2, in order to create the warming energy in the second step, we need an increased devotion. And in step 3 the characteristics of a 'faculty to differentiate', a 'sense of truth' and a 'sense of reality' have their roots in an uprightness force which has been specially schooled by our ego. These three ego activities are of great importance for the transformation of research resistances, and have the potential to develop into higher senses. So we can ascertain that all three faculties are necessary for each step, but in each step the accent is directed to one of the three.

The seven life processes must be transformed into creative faculties, so that it may be possible to go on the way of the third learning path. Additional specific exercises are necessary for every step, in order to awaken within us our slumbering faculties and to create something new.

A description of each of the seven processes for research is given in Chapter 3. They can be seen as steps in a process; however in practice they are in constant movement, interacting. Knowing about them helps orient where you are and what may be overlooked or what still needs to be done.

The forces that corrupt the life processes are described in Chapter 5. The corruptions you may recognize as characteristics of a modern lifestyle. They are evident in our culture. As you approach spiritual thresholds, they become stronger, more visible, and more existential as challenges for inner development. Once seen and recognized, their power changes from adversary to supporter.

Meditative exercises (Chapter 4) are offered for the polarities we encounter on each of the seven processes, to support your inner schooling path and maintain inner balance.

Clearly when we want to bring about changes in the world around us, it must begin with inner changes in oneself. Our spirituality today is earned by our own efforts, developing new faculties out of our own inner forces. What is achieved in this way will have an effect in the future, both for the individual and in the world.

## Overview of the seven research faculties

To give an initial idea of the subject, the seven steps are formulated below and in the table. (They are comprehensively described in Chapter 3.)

| Life processes | Learning processes | Spiritual research path |
| --- | --- | --- |
| 1. breathing | Observation | Encounter and recognize my research question (a questioning observation) |
| 2. warming | Connecting | Creating research warmth through free ego activity |
| 3. nourishing | Spiritual digesting | Finding and going on the path. Method and schooling become one |
| 4. secreting | Individualizing | The answer breaks through out of the other world, and will be researched through independent encounter |
| 5. maintaining | Exercising | Finding the way back to this world and being able to express in words |
| 6. growing | Developing new faculties | An answer grows in this world, becomes earth ripe, checking, applying, making operational |
| 7. reproducing | Creating | Realizing the research results |

Expressed in a context of creativity are the seven steps:

1. What does the world ask from us? Being able to see and read it. Also to see and read the gestures—our observation creativity is now up to the question.
2. Ability to burn up all old stuff in yourself so the juvenile warmth can arise and can become the mirror of the spiritual forces. Creative meditation creates warmth.
3. One now finds the path when all that hinders is being discovered and accepted step by step. This is a creative self-awareness that leads up to the fourth faculty.
4. With deep respect we recognize the key. But the creative force with which one penetrates into the darkness is like a dying and incarnating process. It means to sacrifice oneself into it. It has transformed death into new life. One has to perceive the question, create the warmth medium, go the path, and only then the encounter at the threshold takes place. It is the creative encounter act which creates something new.
5. The path upwards becomes now the path downwards into darkness. What has been spiritually grasped is translated and given form here on earth. But the golden key will be retained. It is a creative, selfless process and mirrors the path upwards, which now becomes the way into darkness.
6. The key seed can now be received, individualized and applied for fellow beings. This demands a social creativity. The juvenile warmth becomes a flame for fellow beings. A new possibility grows; it will be tried out, tested, its reality manifests itself.
7. This mirrors the first step (1), acknowledging what the world asks human beings to do.

One should not hold on to these processes in too strict a manner because they penetrate each other the whole time. One can find the six other procedures in each of them. For example the original question 1 you will find up to the end, step 7, but it changes its meaning in every step. Also the 'warming' penetrates all steps. They show themselves as learning or schooling processes. When you practise them regularly until they become faculties, they can be freely used as seven instruments or processes in researching practice.

It is perhaps useful in studying the seven steps to distinguish between:

- describing the steps, which are necessarily manifold
- schooling the capabilities in order to do the seven steps, and
- describing specific creativity promoting exercises for each of these steps as well as distinguishing between:
- independent learning
- destiny learning, and
- research learning.

## Summary

1. We look for a research question which we are unable to answer without schooling (step 1).
2. This 'unable to answer' is based on an impossibility with which destiny presents us as a learning task in this incarnation (step 2).
3. The overcoming of these specific obstacles creates the healing forces which help us to research the question (step 3).
4. Without these specific obstacles, it would be impossible for us to research this unique question (step 4).

In this way, our destiny is connected with spiritual research.

The questioning, seeking, open, wondering, fundamental attitude becomes nourishment for research learning, and always 'ignited' by the educator through various teaching facilities.

One could consider this creative learning as being much too difficult and not suitable for everyone. Experience shows the opposite: when one has once acquired in a simple way the seven steps and attitudes, one is able to encounter and 'handle' many small questions creatively in daily life. Creative research learning becomes a joy and creates certainty in life. This becomes visible when one once experiences the joy of young people who discover that it is much more wonderful to find breathtaking new questions, to point out new perspectives, than to continuously digest already known learning material which can also be acquired from the Internet.

# 3. The Spiritual Research Process in Seven Steps

## Step 1: Finding the question

The first research process is generally described as perceiving the right research question. This is the transformation of the life process of breathing into our manifold perceiving faculty. Each research process begins with a question—a question which cannot be satisfactorily answered through mere information. What does the world ask from us? Are we able to see and read its gestures? The starting point could be any of the questions one encounters in life and at work that cannot be answered in a satisfactory manner through mere study. The spiritually lazy, lethargic human being stops there; the researcher begins there—researching cognitively, artistically, actively. The first step serves to find this research aim.

In this case a good preparation is to experience the difference between

- information and communication
- knowledge and understanding
- external descriptions and essential experience

We also find indications how to find our research question in those questions which, through the usual information saturation, leave a feeling of disappointment along with abstract general concepts which hurt our sense of truth and our sense of reality.

One can distinguish between four kinds of questions:

1. So-called cognitive questions which appeal to our intellect and feelings.
2. Artistic questions. Each true work of art bears many riddles in its presentation and its creation. Also many hidden secrets and questions live in our social attitudes.

3. Questions of the will, questions of intention within our acting field. These questions often have a moral character.
4. The latter social questions—very deep ones—have often something to do with a personal spiritual path, which we are seeking ourselves. Therefore they can be called existential questions.

They all arise out of encounters with our environment in the broadest and deepest sense—out of encounters with work or vocation, life destiny, the path we are looking for, and nowadays more and more out of encounters with the events of our time. Out of the true questions—not the ones we ponder over out of curiosity—arises the following experience: I have to bring a change within myself in order to find the true, essential answer because my present faculties are in many respects insufficient! This first experience, the recognizing, leads to the next step, warmth creation. Through a real question, our relation to the world undergoes a change. We see and experience everything we encounter in a different manner than previously. It is as if our environment is brightening up. Through theories, concepts, planning, our environment is being surveyed and explained; through new questions, however, it becomes open anew. It is striking which essential questions children are still able to ask, since they have not been saturated with learned answers.

The question arises mainly through a quite specific encounter with a particular situation. Characteristically, this situation is not observed in a usual way, but it becomes transparent for a need or a riddle which is concealed behind it and in fact asks a question itself.

Most people go past the needs of the world. However, now and again one needs to confront them. In the end something has to be answered; it stands in front of us as an urgent task. Through encounter with an actual life situation, an intention that lives unconsciously within us is activated.

Research questions can be very varied—a child whom one does not understand, a patient, an apprentice, a significant work objective, a firm, an initiative—as well as substantial questions such as: What is the origin of fear? What is a shadow, colour, a rainbow? etc. Each spiritual question demands the specific schooling of new faculties which allow one to solve it. In certain cases the question is something that one already brings into this life, concealed in one's biography, and which flashes forth as soon as one encounters it in outer life. Often this kind of question reveals itself in the course of time through feelings of helplessness, illusions, in many blockages—and always in crisis. The decision taken before birth to devote myself to this question is deeply related to my biography.

During the courses on 'spiritual research learning', it often becomes apparent that the chosen questions are the very ones that cannot be researched without transforming the present blockages through schooling work. This has a deep meaning since it is *my* weakness, one-sidedness, incompetence, spiritual/emotion/physical diseases that gives me the possibility to research something unique, which is not available to others. Thus spiritual research is here incorporated in our destiny.

We find out again and again how karma forces give us the opportunity to go on our spiritual research path. It may also become evident what questions you can research, and what not; this is a matter of individual karma. Also different persons will have a different access to the same field.

At this point, the difference from destiny learning emerges. Destiny learning serves the soul development, self-knowledge. Spiritual research, by comparison, serves world needs and questions. My destiny and schooling path devotes itself to objective aims and has in this way a character that is much higher in freedom. We can also omit or neglect it.

How does one transform the life process of 'breathing' into a creative spiritual research force? How do I transform my breathing into a research question? This begins with schooling of attentive observation and discernment.

For this purpose, one lets all 12 senses breath, so that the observation outwards returns to me as an inward question. 'It' looks at me. The research question arises out of the act of facing the environment. A true question is a force, creates a fundamental attitude, becomes a creative faculty which is continuously carried within. It reveals itself then as practising the inner drive to know. It does not leave you alone! When the questioning focus is directed inwards, impressions can rise up that go far beyond just self-knowledge.

## Step 2: Creating research warmth

The second research process is the transformation of the life process of warming to an *ego-active research warming*. This entails looking inward to one's relationship to the question. Where and how does it live in me? What is my relation to it or my love for it? What is my motivation, for what do I do this research? Our 'research warming process' nourishes and accompanies all seven learning and research steps. However, in the second step it is created as a unique activity.

### From juvenile warmth to quintessence

The human being is a warmth being. He can only exist within certain warmth limits. When it is too hot he burns out; when it is too cold he freezes to death. When the body temperature varies from normal, one is ill. The 'warming' life process enables us to exist.

There exists three kinds of warmth:

1. The regulation of the physical warmth of the body.
2. The soul warmth (or coldness) which accompanies our feelings in a manifold manner. We have become acquainted with this kind of warmth already, while going through our independent learning process, as 'interest' and 'connecting'. In destiny learning also, these warming processes appear as special heart impulses. It can also be expressed as an enthusiasm that is situational and is easily excited or diminished.
3. The third form of warmth shows itself as a spiritual activity which has something to do with the spiritual research itself and has a deeper continuity.

Through physical effort, one can warm oneself, but also through spiritual effort. Warmth arising through spiritual effort is independent from the physical body, and arises out of pure spiritual activity. It is actually a self-created warmth. It is also called (by Rudolf Steiner) 'juvenile warmth', which means it is 'warmth created out of nothing'. There are several phenomena accompanying this juvenile warmth, for example dedicated enthusiasm towards a question, the feeling for truth which often has to burn down wrong conceptions or hardened ideas, overcoming resistances and uncertainties, or the faculty to go through and to persevere. The question becomes a motivating force; it does not leave you, but burns within so strong it will overcome outer influences or momentary discouragement.

In the present time, the human being has become passive towards independent spiritual effort, due to various environmental influences. Why should one make efforts for something when one is already able to be informed about everything through an excess of information? Information technology has already undermined to a large extent human communication faculties. As a result of this, encounter faculties dwindle continually. In fact, one of the most difficult and urgent tasks of educators is to work against this culture impairment in our schooling processes. Out of the 'answer culture' an open questioning culture must be born again. But in this case we need spiritual effort, a spiritual-research warmth producing creativity!

Most people have been carrying within themselves already for a long time, usually half-consciously, many true-life questions. An apparently logical argument is that one can also avoid a lot of effort and leave others to find out. Spiritual answers to fundamental questions inevitably come back to warmth capacity in dealing with this step, because this becomes here even more existential. The Rosicrucians were acquainted with this newly arising warmth through their alchemical work, calling it a fifth element, adding to earth, water, air (ether) and fire. With this fifth element, the quintessence, one could penetrate everything since it has an effect on the threshold between the physical/sensual/material and spiritual/transcendental life and immaterial. It is evident that one must use such a quintessence when one wants to research with one's own spiritual forces in order to bring about a new creation. This force produces, in fact, a research force with which one can transform the warming process of the etheric body.

As step 2 of the research process this warmth activity is meditatively, inwardly applied to the question, with the help of my sense of truth. The question is explored in my own relationship to it, in three ways:

1. *How is the question composed? What do the words contain?* Is my question really an open question or do hidden conditions, judgements, laws, conclusions, assumptions, habitually applied methods, etc. interfere? Conflict between my sense of truth and the formulation of the question found by me will now arise, and during this time many accustomed concepts will be seen to be irrelevant.

2. *What is my relationship to the field of my question? How does it touch my life now? Where does it take me?*
Why and what is the point of the question I have chosen? The warmth efforts are now directed inwards and a confrontation with my self takes place. Note that many questions are in fact self-knowledge questions and belong then to 'destiny learning', which is another process. This does not mean that research learning has nothing to do with karma, only the aim orientation is different. Spiritual research is always at the service of fellow beings. We look for an answer which brings something new in the world, which can be understood, used and further developed. Karma work itself provides many questions, which have to be answered so that this work may become accessible to many others. However, self-knowledge is in the first place useful to me alone, whereas spiritual research serves the world where we are living and out of this attitude arises my real burning question.

3. *Do I have a question directed to the world or to my environment, or does my life situation question me? What is my moral motivation for this research quest?*
This is a strong challenge towards my self-created research

warmth. On the one hand, the question arose out of a true encounter with the environment, an individual question, thus it belongs to my destiny. However, must I answer this question? What do I want to serve with this research? Is a call sent to my creative research faculty? I must create something new; there is no point in repeating something else. Can I try? Should I try? Should I not formulate my question in another way? Perhaps my haughtiness is misleading me? and so on. It is an existential self-confrontation.

All friends who have endeavoured to pursue a modern research path know this as a momentary desperation—since how can one from the beginning know whether one has the capabilities, the possibilities and sufficient creative warmth force to really create something new? All the same, one has created this research warmth oneself through the transformation of physical and soul warmth ... So why should one be unable to go further? 'I like the one who longs for the impossible,' said a well-known German! The new adult learning educator has the duty to accompany creatively every student during such a 'powerlessness' crisis.

After many research experiences, one knows that powerlessness experiences (being without old powers) belong to creative research processes. Only with a spiritual effort which produces renewed warming can this powerlessness be converted into new experiences, ideas, insights, etc. Everything old within myself must die when something new wants to be born. It is an ability to burn down everything old within me, so that juvenile warmth may arise and may become a mirror for heavenly powers. Creative meditation creates warmth. The warmth medium we create carries the further processes of the research.

Thus it is necessary to discover the new, self-created force and to bring it to life, because it is actually unbearable to leave the true question unanswered. It is like a desperation experience. It can even become an undignified human experience, a self-defeat, a sort of spiritual suicide.

This and similar testing should now penetrate and warm

the question and make out of it the selfless relationship: *I become my question. I accept that I am myself the instrument of the question.*

## Step 3: Going on the path and transforming resistances

Having deepened our research question in step 1 and become more conscious of our aim in step 2, we now strive for creativity in 'knowing', and seeking in particular the knowledge our question demands from us. We are not only the research instrument for it, but we must also re-educate ourselves into this particular research instrument and thus be able to acquire new knowledge. Because we are the mediating instrument, our own experiences are part of the material to be studied. Hence an honesty and objectivity towards oneself is a necessary spirit-ego faculty for this step. The nature of the question could take us on a long journey or quest, into many different fields of study, or artistic activities, or observation in practical life, or special schooling processes. There is no recipe for 'the way' as this depends on the source behind the question, what kind of question it is, and on the person doing the research.

*Step 3 is the transformation of what is called nourishment as a life process.* Of course it is not physical nourishment that is meant here, but spiritual nourishment. At this point we pursue an unusual and new path which, through the transformation of everything that prevents us finding solutions and answers, must lead us to new abilities regarding this. My life and my spiritual path are now led by my question. Inner path choices are also led by the need for new faculties to pursue my question. We not only want an 'answer', we are on a pathway to a new level where the 'answer' lives.

Thus step 3 presents itself as a double process in that it consists of going on the path and transforming my resistances. The transformation process is also a spiritual nourishment.

The life process 'nourishment' has the force to transform

substance so that it nourishes our organism. A similar expression is 'transsubstantiation'. The researcher must achieve this himself on his research path in the way that he carries this question in himself, and *transforms himself into an adequate research instrument* with the help of his self-renewed warmth/ego activity.

Thus it can happen that out of the idea that 'I am the research instrument' arises 'I am not already a research instrument' because the past holds me in its grip. I experience the gap between present state and future necessity. Now the aim of the question must be kindled again so that the next step flashes up out of the question. The question summons me; my one-sidedness hinders me, and the movement in between releases me for the next step. My habitual way of researching, as well as the results of past researches, obstruct my way. My ego in its creative energy releases me. As soon as I begin to move again everything becomes easier.

A specific question has also specific blockages. Therefore the specific blockages which I neglected up to now are to be worked upon and overcome, so that I may be able to explore my specific question. Such blockages can be concepts, traditional views, methods and fixed notions, and can also arise out of artistic habits or even moral principles. Most of the time it is a mixture of all these.

Now a new field of tension arises between my individual disposition and my self-created research aim—namely the 'why', 'what is the point' or 'for whom' of the research question, of which I became aware during the second warmth step. This inner field of tension between my disposition and my aspiration is a precondition and source of nourishment leading to the so-called 'Aha' experience, presentiments, intuitive acts, etc. In this struggle between aim, schooled conditions and one-sidedness, our ambition or aspiration can beguile us into making uncontrolled leaps, fantasies, assumptions and associations, or lead to conditioning in method fixations, concept autism and model restrictions. How should one cope with this struggle, which everyone who is determined to research has to go through? Meanwhile, in each step one must be capable of leaving all securities behind and go into the uncertain future.

Through our efforts to transform blockages, we open the space to perceive anew. The activity and effort widens our vision. The world begins to show us what we had not noticed before. You may feel you are being helped by some invisible forces—for instance, unusual events are presented to you, a book appears which you are drawn towards, a person makes a comment totally unaware how significant their comment is for you, you find yourself in a place you did not plan to be in and encounter just what you needed to hear. We are given signs and hints how to go further and must learn to watch for them. Further, you may feel surroundings are becoming light, you see more clearly. Or you may find darkness instead of light. It is important not to flee from these darker places but to observe them and their effect with a questioning, researching attitude: 'What is the message?'

Often these incidents do not seem outwardly to have anything to do with my research; but in fact it does so inwardly. The impression arises that the path is guided and that I am taken seriously from the other side. I experience support when I take myself seriously with my question and when my research warmth makes me more and more a research instrument. These and similar fundamental feelings nourish our spiritual perception and develop our inner and outer vigilance. Regular reflection-breaks are necessary in this case, through which also egoistic and egocentric characteristics, up to ego-mania, can be discovered.

The tension between my research limits and my research aim remains until I enter into the unknown. My aim leads me and my transformed movement nourishes me when I have broken down (digested) my blockages. The inner research resistances may present themselves as if they are outer research resistances. The temptation remains, however, namely this losing of oneself in endless detours or in associative leaps which go beyond the essential schooling of new capabilities. *One learns with time to find a creative middle between what the aim is asking and what my own 'what I have become' demands.*

Those who have read and studied the books *Practising Destiny* and *The Threefold Path of Destiny Learning* have had the opportunity to discover that the true decision to research something new can already influence future destiny in a considerable manner. Through a question process operating within myself, I can already see my environment in another way. I have other encounters and other inner experiences.

There has been much psychological research about the particular circumstances in which creative events can appear. Here, for the learning process, only one of them will be mentioned: the experience of 'helplessness', which does not move forward in spite of energetic mental effort. This is experienced as 'hopelessness'. This bundled energy must now be held back, left to night consciousness, to waiting calmly and unperturbed. The next day a creative research force can arise out of the lameness. Many researchers use this so-called night learning as an important and supporting help. What we are unable to see clearly in day consciousness is taken further during sleep where we are in another world. Our daytime efforts are transformed by the night process into new insights and new faculties—a reinforcing process of earthly and spiritual worlds. Putting a question to the night is a valuable research methodology.

Practising this creative middle again and again leads to a new experience. The spirit or essence of the question becomes itself the manager or guide, which demands again a new faculty and leads to it at the same time. This step of the research process produces the spiritual nourishment we need in order to encounter individually the cosmic spiritual revelation on the threshold in step 4.

Unless one takes the path upwards towards the next step by gradually transforming on the way every failure, every illusion within oneself, step 5 cannot really take place (which means maintaining what was discovered in step 4, the breakthrough). In step 3 the danger of making leaps must therefore be overcome, otherwise difficulties arise later. When the earth gravity of one's instrument is not transformed, the acquired spirit (4) cannot be maintained (5), and cannot be permanent and continuous.

## Ways of reinforcing our sense of truth

There are three levels of our sense of truth which should always accompany the seven steps:

1. *Presuppositions*

We presume a connection and explanation of an idea ... there is no certainty yet but a possibility only. One must leave everything open, since it could still become something completely different. There are many of these presumptions and they are important, since they might lead to something quite new. The presumptions are in our thinking and imagining, inspired by fantasy.

2. *Premonitions*

Premonitions go much deeper and arise out of our tentative feeling of truth. Here we should not constrain and harden them into absolute certainties. This tentative perceiving, feeling of truth should be retained; stay open to each premonition that occurs.

3. *Certainties*

They can arise slowly, but can also appear quite suddenly with an almost existential steadfast quality. Such certainty has something to do with our intuitive will and should therefore be taken seriously. A well-known experience is 'I know that it is like that but I cannot quite understand it yet'. Then one has to wait until it matures so far that it can be communicated to others and be confirmed in practice. Here one has also to do with our level of knowledge. At a certain level something can be right and true. In spite of it there is always a still higher and deeper truth behind it. The knowledge that one is always on the path to truth creates a healthy sense of truth.

These short hints may be enough to help the researcher—each time he believes he has found something—to school the ability to differentiate, in connection with the three ways, how his feeling of truth can express itself and develop.

The aim is to develop one's own faculty of knowing, by which the truth speaks and is obvious, needing no other empirical evidence or proof.

## Step 4: Encountering the breakthrough

The fourth step stands in the middle of the seven research processes. It shows a central event during which our hitherto daily acquired intelligence encounters a sort of 'essence' experience, as an insight into our question. There can be many names for this causal event, such as breakthrough, threshold event, inspiration, 'Aha' experience, intuition, a quite new idea flashes up, etc. The essential thing, however, is that a true encounter takes place between our healthy human understanding and sense of truth and a spiritual element, coming as close as possible to the reality, to what it *is*.

Generally this step is experienced as a special moment of awareness or presence, transcending our usual consciousness. All the past has led up to it, the future is born into it, the space is open to receive it. The moment is timeless.

A new kind of creativity arises out of the encounter. Something new is born out of it. This was the case in every step, but now a turning point is also achieved. Hitherto we had looked for an answer; now we find something new, creative, which arises out of the encounter itself. This encounter is therefore the turning point. What has been here discovered, however, must still be made understandable, communicable, applicable, and finally reconstructable for others. It has been spiritually discovered, but must be made mature for earth and mankind (by steps 5, 6, 7).

At this point a fundamental scientific law asserts itself, i.e. a new discovery in research must be understandable, communicable, applicable and reconstructable before it can be recognized. The educator who schools these research faculties should be able to represent this moral fundamental attitude. There are today many quasi-scientific assertions which result from personal experiences, premonitions, transcendental breakthroughs, but where a clear account of the path and how these discoveries have been found have been omitted. This moral fundamental requirement is naturally a basic condition for all learning and knowledge processes. However, it is in this 'threshold situation', with its material/transcendental character, that most mistakes are made. The emphasis that this should be an *encounter between two worlds* is the modern aspect of creative research learning.

It is the drama of autonomy! Can I retain my researching, exploring, independent activity when immaterial essences, demonic elements in the form of delusions, haughtiness, arrogance or things of this kind may take hold of me? Can I maintain that an encounter takes place on the threshold between spirit essence and individual research? When this is successful, the following happens out of this fundamental attitude:

My own I encounters spirit essence
And individualizes spirit essence in me!

When you read biographies of well-known scientists, you always come across these breakthrough moments. This is then named 'inspiration' or 'intuition'. The statement is often offered, 'I know that it is real but I cannot quite understand it yet.' One does not necessarily encounter the essence of the question; however, an encounter takes place with the spiritual world in which many elements can be involved. The insights will be as great or small as the person is at this time able to carry. It can happen in a flash and last a lifetime. It is always something spiritual that one encounters. Therefore, the sense of truth (with enhanced discernment) must be present during the encounter. Everything depends on whether you are still imprisoned in your senses or past knowledge, or whether you meet independently and are capable of discerning. When this is not successful or only partially so, it is recommended to postpone going further or to repeat the experiment at a later date. The main thing is to be able to hold your balance and ego-centred consciousness between both worlds.

There is a particular source of illusions to be observed among clairvoyants who experience spiritual visions. The experience itself could be quite genuine, but its interpretation may not reflect reality when it is not based on the indivi-dualized, exploring, fundamental attitude mentioned above. The temptation is to receive this event as a revelation purely from the higher worlds, as was often done in the Middle Ages. Our task now is to maintain the attitude of a real, modern researcher.

Up to this point, the schooling of research faculties has been described as being in seven different steps. This is necessary because they have to be differentiated for our schooling purposes. However, in the daily practice of research they often occur spontaneously, and not in the same sequence. Since we find ourselves now in the fourth step—a substantial middle point—it is helpful to describe certain variations which may occur.

Breakthrough experiences occur almost daily, only we are not aware of them or do not pay enough attention to them. If we do observe them, we often do not know how to deal with them, since they are not logical or appear as illogical asso-ciations. It often happens that one is not in a well-balanced state, or is half dreaming or busy with other items, or one awakens suddenly during the night with an answer. If we school ourselves more and more to take these breakthroughs seriously—which is very important—questions then arise as to how these experiences are to be evaluated. Here a few examples:

1. The experiences can be fully conscious as has already been described—a breakthrough for the solution of my question. A distraction which may then occur, and which is well known to the author, is the immediate appearance of a further question which one wants to explore straight away—you forget that at this very point three steps have already been made and one cannot abruptly leap from one research path to the next one.

2. Such an experience might not even be a breakthrough; it can just be a hint for the research path that has been trod up to now. The temptation can occur that one believes oneself to

be already on the fourth step. Present-day science often commits this error and draws conclusions without encountering the essential spirit at the threshold in step 4. Honest researchers say then, fittingly, it is a provisional hypothesis—but is one then allowed to apply it in human life? A weighty moral question!

3. The experience can be a pictorial vision, an inspired element or an intuitive premonition. You can often have an impression of reality without yet quite understanding the meaning. Then it is necessary to repeat the earlier steps in a serious manner up to the threshold encounter described above. Holding back and waiting are now indicated—a sort of creative resignation.

4. Furthermore there are innumerable experiences that are hints along the path (as mentioned above in step 3). Many researchers experience this as secondary phenomena along their path. The awareness of my research question has already an affect, so that I judge everything I encounter on the path in a different manner and the research warmth motivates me to explore further. It is a kind of nourishment, an encouragement to pursue the path.

5. Along this research path a kind of digestion process occurs between spiritual and soul fields. This prepares us for the encounter described in step 4, with a heightened awareness.

Each step schools us for the next one. Therefore it may happen that one observes that it is necessary to look back once again, for example in order to deepen the research question once more, because the ego warmth was not sufficient to close up a gap in step 3, etc. When step 4 is experienced as a changing and turning point, it is appropriate to look back once again at the path you have gone up to now. Then you become conscious that every step was a particular process in itself and has awakened different new creative faculties. It is important to write down the essential aspect of each step in order to reconstruct the path that one has trodden, to discover gaps and to become aware of the mistaken possibilities which have been described. This 'assessment' is therefore very important—as one will notice later—because the following three steps 5, 6 and 7 mirror the three first steps. Mistakes on the upward path become blockages on the downward path.

Finally, here are a few comments on the difference between 'learning to learn as an adult' and 'creative spiritual research learning'. Unlike usual learning, spiritual learning has another time dimension. Everyone can discover this when trying to plan his spiritual research within an apparent period of time. The concepts 'spiritual' and 'creativity' do not lend themselves to being quantitatively determined. Our clock time is a violation of spiritual reality, because our need for certainty wants to make everything quantitatively measurable. When you do a review over the first four steps, you discover soon that spiritual perceptions, creative moments, breakthroughs, but also blockages, follow living rhythmic processes. In addition, long-term effort, waiting, almost forgetting or sudden solutions belong also to these processes. It is as if something needs time to mature within us. It can be past experience which is presenting itself in quite different aspects, or the question comes up 'Why did I not understand this earlier?'

Endless examples could be mentioned in order to describe how the life processes operate in us in a rhythmic manner, with spiritual creativity. It is important to find out which rhythms are important to me in my research question, or how to handle day and night rhythms. Also, how do I make progress; when should I make efforts on a spiritual level and when should I restrain myself? When and how should I move between mind work, artistic creative exercises, acting tests, and more contemplation on the deeper sense of the research? No time instructions should be given here, since each must find his own rhythm. It is important then to act with complete consciousness of all inner and outer processes during the first four steps.

To our amazement, quite unforeseen incidents occur that provide important hints for what one presently needs. Often these incidents do not seem outwardly to have anything to do with my research; however it does in fact do so inwardly. In the threshold encounter the being of the question does not always show itself immediately, but it shows nevertheless an encounter with the supersensible world, where many beings could be involved. It is a spiritual reality that one encounters. The impression arises that the path is guided and that I am taken seriously from the other side. I experience support when I take myself seriously with my question and when my research warmth makes me more and more a research instrument. These and similar fundamental feelings nourish our spiritual perception and develop our inner and outer vigilance.

## Step 5: Translating the new idea into human language

This is in fact a question of communication, but not merely of information as is usually done in research fields. It becomes nowadays more and more difficult to conceive the life process of 'maintaining' in adequate words, since language is increasingly undermined and often used in an immeasurably superficial manner.

During the learning processes the life process of 'maintaining' was converted into 'rhythmical exercising' to develop and maintain new faculties. In research we are concerned with an essential threshold encounter, now changed in order to *translate* our discovery to an encounter with human listeners through an *understandable communication*. Every researcher knows how often breakthroughs get lost again when one has not immediately written them down, that is, one has not 'maintained' them. When breakthroughs in step 4 occur during the night, which often happens, it becomes particularly difficult. A notebook and writing tools beside the bed brings a possible solution in this case. Also when the breakthrough takes place during the day, often unexpectedly in the form of a passing thought while we are busy with something completely different, it has to be maintained. However the question is not yet solved until the discovery has been described in understandable human communication. Even scientific jargon can be a blockage to our understanding. The dilemma is how to put it into words without losing its living substance, or killing it in the process.

The breakthrough or spiritual experience may be very real and alive for you; and you may be able to describe your experience. But this does not yet mean it is applicable in any other sphere. The temptation is to leap to sharing or applying it, and then one is disappointed if it does not take root or perhaps is not understood. There are worlds behind your words which another cannot know. Some insights are still tender, very new, and if shared too soon their forces are dissipated or lost. They need to be inwardly nurtured until more secure and alive in you. Another possibility for 'maintaining' however is to share with another, and help to incarnate it by speaking it. Here one must choose with whom to speak where its tender newness will be respected and clearly heard, perhaps even questioned to check its reality or context. Part of 'translating' is to sense the life sphere of the insight, where does it belong, for whom.

An important faculty to support this step is artistic or aesthetic feeling. It is an art to give expression to the invisible, which always has been the task of arts throughout history.

From the spiritual side we are dealing with realities of word, of being, of knowing, of moral forces. In translating it is difficult to find adequate earthly terms to say it, to be it, to know or understand it to be real.

Here, day/night learning is a help! In 'learning from the night' it is described how every night our etheric body repeats the counterpart of day impressions in living thought forms. It is visible there how our daytime fragment belongs in the universal all. Our efforts to encounter the reality, our progress so far, is reinforced during sleep and affirmed or corrected. Our meagre language effort sounds with the cosmic word, and individualizes it. In this way, gradually our human language can be filled with substance and meaning. Here we find the source in order to school the faculties of step 5. The night work of the etheric body encompasses also the maintaining process.

Sometimes, for instance, one has gathered a number of 'fragments' and one day, out of the night, there is a synthesis.

It all falls into place—now you have it and you know it. This synthesis will come in its own time, not by your demands! If we find a new true insight and can express it in words or actions, others will recognize its reality. It is 'obvious' or accessible to healthy common sense. It may be first expressed in the form of an imagination, in which—as Rudolf Steiner uses the term—the image contains its spiritual meaning. It will only later become applicable in practice.

Here is another example. When the insight is for a new exercise, it will eventually be effective because there is a spiritual archetype behind it. The giver and participants will recognize it, because it will work in a special way. For such a research question, trying out in practice is part of the research method in step 3. The researcher observes his experiences, which give a medium for discovering new insights. The final result comes about then in steps 5, 6 and 7, after preparing the way in step 3 by 'playing with' creative ideas.

Something very important arises when the three successive steps can be explored and experienced as a coherent unity. We are concerned here with the following steps, respectively:

Step 3    going on the research path
Step 4    carrying out the threshold encounter
Step 5    creating communication among human beings

At first these three aims appear to be in opposition to each other when considered superficially. Step 3 demands a transformation of old into new, related research faculties. Step 5 demands the creating of human communication regarding this. Step 4 finds itself between the two and appears like a deed and has the character of a balancing centre between the two. Thus steps 3 and 5 no longer appear like opposing elements, but as polarities which should encounter each other at the centre. A further consideration of this polarity shows that the researcher has stored within himself a lot of what he has acquired in the course of his life as 'faculties' or 'knowledge'. It is like a 'possessing'. He has now to give up these 'stored faculties' in order to acquire new ones. Past 'habits' have to be transformed into innovative acting and knowing. It may seem easy, but traditional research methods show that old models stick deeply in our organism.

Step 5—the third step in our reflection—shows other, almost opposite, features. Here we have to do with a *spiritual* transformation. Countless conceptions in our language habits have become abstract; the meaning has undergone changes, becoming hard, empty. Much concept autism and fixed ideas can be found in the language used by scholars, civil servants and even educators. That models hardly correspond with reality nowadays is a great hindrance for many true researchers.

However a living dynamic process now arises. To the degree the researcher is transformed into a research instrument, can create a new way of communicating it. Also both mirror each other—in so far as an encounter between earthly and cosmic intelligence has taken place. Here we feel again the night work of our etheric body which can accompany this mirroring. The transformation of our research instrument is more day work. Inspiration and revival of language is largely etheric night work.

To convert the experience out of step 4 into human language in step 5 is only possible when you have not only understood the prior steps but have endured and transformed them within yourself. They have become experience and nourishment. Indications of your path which made the result possible may be expressed in simple words, clear, effective and enlightened. The essence, which often has an ideal character, is important, while detailed accounting may be rather disturbing to the listener.

**Further remarks on transforming the past and creating something new—carrying out the encounter in the middle**
This is the dynamic of the research path. The essence turns out to be the basis of a new creativity. This kind of research can hardly be found in the Middle Ages. We will see later that step 2, the self-created warming, mirrors itself and finds its complement in step 6 'making it useable and applicable'. Step 1 'finding my research question' at the beginning finds its

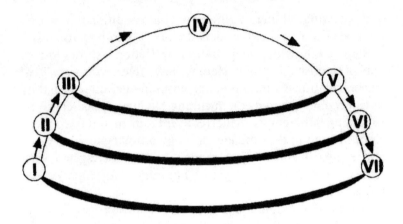

answer in step 7 'making it applicable, reproducible', at the end of the process.

It is good to bring to one's mind that we are on the way to realize on earth something new, which arose out of the encounter. The last three steps are shortly mentioned:

- making it communicable
- making it practicable and workable
- making it reproducible and reconstructable

Although it sounds easy, it demands again new creative faculties in practice. A lot of research work gets lost when these three following steps are disregarded. Since every researcher's faculties are limited, support from experienced colleagues can be enormously important. For educators, the students are often the best advisors in this respect. The first four steps reveal a strong individualizing character, while the last three are based on an increasingly selfless cooperation up to the realization in step 7.

The transformation of basic attitudes towards a new way of learning is a great ideal.

- 'What must I do to make the threshold encounter possible?'
- 'What is the world demanding from me so that it can create a progressive and healthy development for my fellow human beings?

Here by means of a research learning a synthesis of scientific, artistic and moral elements can be recognized. It should be clear that these three elements have always to be cultivated in adult learning. Also in regard to those who do research as a profession, one must endure inner conscience struggles in connection with the aims and applications of the research—a situation which I myself had to endure.

## Step 6: Making the new idea ripe for application

The sixth life process of 'growing' is the life force of development in the human being. In the biography this is expressed in archetypal phases of life. We grow or ripen, we mature as a human being. The life process 'growing' should now be transformed into the faculty of *making the research seed practicable, workable*. The growing step is not the final aim of research, but only a step along the path in order to make that which has been discovered ripe for the earth. When is the right time? If it is too soon it will wither or fade away because not enough substance is in it. Is the environment well enough prepared for it? Application in life requires being ready to identify with and give one's life forces to bring the insight alive in the world, not only within oneself.

This step means transposing our maintaining context: *learning to practise the understood idea*. A characteristic feature of step 5 was to make the newly created understandable for our fellow beings. Now in step 6 the point is to find out how to make the newly understood and understandable suitable and workable for others. This means testing it in practice, trying out prototypes, finding its useful context or situation, what can be used at this time and how. It asks for a development of 'moral technique' to be able to integrate the new discovery into today's reality. Time is also important, in how far is it ripe enough, too early, too late. That means growing is a process of growth *and* decay.

Application addresses itself to our will and our deeds. Growing as a life process shows a natural organic course.

When our body, for example, is unable to grow in an organic and rhythmic manner but is influenced by involuntary forces in its growth, modern (cancerous) diseases arise. Already in the transforming process, of growing forces into new faculties, it is observed that hardening arises in the etheric body when growing forces are converted into automatic skills.

A similar impairment can occur while transforming the life process 'growing' into making the new idea suitable and practical for daily reality. It is, however, difficult to become aware of this immediately, since this impairment is considered as normal, as a secondary phenomenon accompanying the development of consciousness of self.

First an example for this effect: no young person is satisfied with physical growing only. He wants to grow as a personality, to become somebody, to achieve something, to be praiseworthy and in this way to intensify his 'self-consciousness' as much as he can. This urge, which should grow in a rhythmic, organic manner, can also degenerate into an unhealthy 'ripening' through an over-estimating of self. That is a maladjustment, a blockage which can be easily overlooked but which has to be transformed. The maxim of our modern culture 'as much success as possible with as little effort as possible' is in this case not very helpful. The temptation to apply this principle in the step 'earthly realization of the new idea' is very strong and represents a blockage.

The second blockage arises out of imitation. One reads about a new idea and believes oneself able to practise it immediately, before becoming familiar with the elements expressed in it. Just as in adult education, only superficially understood elements are often imitated during the application of new ideas, thus losing the essence. The many highly praised standard seminars and educative courses testify to this. However, it is clear that the practical execution of true new ideas demands new faculties. Many new creations have already dropped out of sight again because of too hasty growth. However, the living nature says there is also a rhythmic process of growth and decline.

It is not easy to give general valid indications about this process, because the applications of true new elements are so numerous and also so different from one another. However, there are a few general rules.

Testing, trying out, experimenting before handing over something for execution has been a traditional practice since time immemorial. Unfortunately, this process is often ignored and reduced to whether the application brings the results that have been promised in the theory. The *actual consequence* for the consumer who regularly uses the new element often remains unchecked and therefore unknown.

One example: the influence of the use of computers, Internet and multi-media techniques on our mental creative faculties has hardly been examined. We touch here on the moral aspect of creative research. In step 5 artistic creativity was demanded for finding a new creative language. Here in step 6 moral qualities are imperative in the application of the new element. We need the consciousness that everything new that we create is used by our fellow beings and thus evokes affects. Consequences follow! The educator who aims at developing creative research faculties in fellow beings should become more and more aware that these faculties have to embody the synthesis of scientific, artistic and moral components. This is true for each of the 7 steps, but here this moral component is especially clearly visible in the application of the totally new.

Here step 6 is a mirror of step 2 where we examined our inner moral motivation towards the question, and became the instrument for the research. Now in bringing the newly created into daily life here on earth, one has to bring oneself to a moral earth maturity. I become aware that my individual creativity leads to consequences for our earthly life world— healing, helping, creating the future or disturbing, ailing, destroying. The validity of the individual research is proven in practice, to be a valid contribution to humanity or to the world. The individual ego tries now to act out of free deeds in the situation, practising the new found understanding, free of an earth-bound or karmic-bound past. The fire of the independent spirit from step 2 radiates through the upright individual towards the world.

In the same way the creative educator should also be aware of the strong impact on the minds of people by educational conditioning. He should mobilize his own creative faculties in order to foster an independent, individualized adult learning and a moral responsibility as is aimed for in this research work.

## Step 7: Realizing the new idea

As this step is a transformation of the life process of 'reproduction', we remind the reader of Chapter 1 in this book on what is meant by creativity.

Just as the first step was a beginning, the last step is an end, and demands therefore also very different research faculties. The creative beginning and the creative end are extreme antitheses. Just as the finding of the true question can be experienced as a birth process, so can the realizing be felt as a death process, a parting, a letting go, ending by handing over, etc. It is, however, clear that this last step demands the *faculty of forming*, such as the last brush strokes of a painting, the summary of an article, the irrevocable composition of a book, the final part of a symphony, yes even the parting address for a deceased friend. The art of forming is the ability to create a form that holds the life seed and has not killed the essence.

It is striking in this researching-forming ability that an audience is always present as a receiver. Creating something new is finally a deed that has brought a change in the world, whether big or small. The created form can be designed in such a way that nobody becomes aware of what is new; in contrast, it can cause striking reactions or create a great number of other effects. Could it even be harmful if simply copied and used? What will be the consequences? Is it the right time and the right way to place this in the world? Our faculty of 'moral technique' becomes essential.

We can be sure that our deeds are written into the earth's history; on the human will or deed level there is a continuity for the earth. There is also a continuity for our own karma in future consequences for the shaping of our destiny.

Now it becomes clear how the last and first step mirror each other. With the finding of my personal question the future was born, which was only possible when I was able to let go within myself of what belonged to the past, what has been already created. Now at the end I must be able to carry out what has been created—the result—in such a way that something new can arise for my fellow beings. Therefore an element of selflessness is required; I must also be inwardly changed, able to create anew in every situation out of this newly created material in me.

A very important fundamental attitude is always to renew. All creative research elements should be of use for our fellow beings. It has not only to do with the content of what has been discovered, but also making it possible that seeds for the 'new' are laid in the souls of the observers. When one bears this aim in oneself in form-giving, a lot has already been won. The moral element, which should penetrate everything, is especially considered at this point.

The outer presentation of the new idea could appear as a completed process, but this is not always the case. Rather it may be, for example, notices on a page in an incomplete form of configuration, or still a hotchpotch of colours and lines, or a meticulously noted number of words, eventually also spoken words, etc. If one would simply reproduce such a presentation nothing new could arise out of it, but only an imitation of the outline. When the receiver recognizes this outline as an artistic work, something new can arise out of it. He brings then what has been presented to a resurrection within himself and in this way it becomes original in itself. It is the realized final point of a long sevenfold research path. It dies in its form and is now accessible to every human being who can bring it back to life. The life element has continuity.

This means that in fact an encounter occurs in each of the seven steps. In this last step, however, it is an encounter between the researcher and the person who can now recognize and realize this new idea.

It can thus also be born as a seed of the 'new' within the observer. In this last case it is the creativity of the researcher which lights up the seed of the 'new' within the observer, through his form-shaping. For the researcher it is a dying along his research path. For the receiver on the contrary it is a new birth. The 'die and become' was actually a fundamental element in each of the steps, for otherwise no creativity could have been born; but there was also a following step. Now these two fundamental elements are separated into the creative spiritual research and observation of the result. It 'dies' for the researcher and is born 'new' as a seed for the user.

Sometimes it is only much later that the world is ready to receive a new creation and it can be actually realized. At first it may be only accessible as an imagination, which gradually penetrates to the level of application—perhaps over two or three generations, or for social impulses after 33 years. If this step is done with sufficient 'moral technique', however, this means the ripeness of the environment is also taken into account in the form it is given. One does what is possible at the time.

The whole process presents itself as a totality, with the three upward steps up to the encounter process at the threshold and the three downward steps back down to earth ripening. When we can affirm, after having regularly schooled these seven creative steps, that the predisposition to creative spiritual research learning is present in every human being, then we can also affirm that it belongs to human nature to school these faculties. Moral urge, artistic work and researching scientific truth unite themselves then into a wholeness in creative spiritual research learning.

At this point we have to name a few *resistances* which may arise in the creative form-giving.

1. One is unable to come to a completion because one always discovers something new. Each step opens again a further horizon pointing out something new. Out of creative action grows a kind of nascent desire, which has to be transformed into a rounding off or an initiative for our fellow beings.

2. Desire to achieve perfection. Many artists and scientists suffer from this, especially when appropriate talents exist. Special genius faculties which one has, identify themselves with our ego. The brilliancy is often not acquired but has been brought into life as a 'given'. Then when one explores something new, one has the urge to present it in a perfect manner. A creative research process in its nature is never perfect but a continuous one. Simplifying and restraining throws up new questions in the observer; perfection summons a feeling of shame and being incapable. To be able to strive for a creative resignation is an important talent for every educator.

3. The tendency of the researcher to display everything, up to every aspect, every detail and point of view. The researcher gets so absorbed in his process that he does not find the space to distil the essence. Extreme simplification on the contrary causes superficiality in the observer and the essence gets lost.

A remaining question: Is this 'new' born in step 4, or first in the 'realization step'? One could perhaps say in the spirit of the researcher that it arose in step 4; for fellow beings, however, it arose only in step 7 when it has become an earth-ripe deed.

## Developing the seven creative research faculties

When polarities meet they will develop the relevant creative faculties.

**General exercise:** Past encounters future/Future encounters past

**1 Breathing**    My ego                                           My environment

My ego meets my environment and out of this arises my research question. My environment also meets me and creates the question in me, and in the encounter of both the essential research question will be born.

**2 Warming**    My ego                                           My research question

My ego meets my research question and out of this develops research warmth. I am now the research question and I become the research instrument

**3 Nourishing**    The creative researcher                        The research resistances

I as research instrument meet my research resistances. The transformation of my resistances creates the spiritual nourishment on the way

**4 Individualizing**    The spiritual achieved                    The spiritual essence

The spiritual research meets the spiritual essence and this creates a new reality as germ of becoming a reality on earth

**5 Maintaining**

The new germ                                      Human language

The new germ needs human language and creates the human understanding. The germ becomes human

**6 Growing**

The humanized idea                       The reality of the earth

The humanized idea meets the earthly reality and creates earthly maturity so that every human being can use it

**7 Reproducing**

The realized idea                           The realized form

The realized idea meets the realized form and dies in the form, but will be newly born in those who will use it

# 4. Exercises for Developing Research Faculties

The primary intent in these exercises is schooling the inner faculties and attitudes needed for spiritual research and creative action. The exercises work with polarity and 'the middle' so that the human being finds its inner upright centre. They aim to open an inner awareness of the etheric life stream, in the invisible sphere of life itself.

## Nature of the exercises

Meditative words are accompanied by hand gestures. The gestures are at first outer movements but in carrying them out they become transformed to inner movement. Eurythmy exercises can be an important support for developing inner movement and a relation to the etheric life stream.

Essential in meditative work is to penetrate through the outer word form to the invisible forces and qualities that lie behind the words. One can experience in these exercises that the movement frees the words into another dimension of space, so they are more alive, and one is more aware of time elements, as in past/present/future consequences. Working only with the words is of course possible, but its effect may be one-sided, staying in the head sphere. Since the seven different life processes are behind the words for each of the seven exercises, the movement naturally adjusts to the word content. Words without movement have no life; we bring dead words alive through our outer and inner movement.

The form of the movements has freedom inherent in it. 'I as ego do it, creating a seed force in me in the open space for a new faculty to grow.'

The medium of the exercises is working with polarities, creating a tension between them and a working sphere in which to arrive at the 'essential middle'. It needs practice to reach the 'essential middle' and be able to hold this. The medium also may bring to awareness blockages which are to be transformed on the way.

No one can give you your forces or faculties. Reading about the exercises and debating intelligently will achieve nothing. You are yourself the researcher and the instrument. You find your own way in the doing and becoming. The research attitude is also being schooled by how you deal with and observe your own experiences.

## Results of the exercises

The effect is to find a centre in yourself, bringing you closer to the earthly side of the research questioning process and to cosmic and invisible sources as well.

The exercises are done independently of any actual research question you are working with. But an effect may be observed, such as better clarity, or a new orientation, or increased intuitive ability. The exercises are unusual, different from other kinds of exercises, since they are aimed at individual activity and development, in support of one's own spiritual path.

The individuality becomes through this ever more present in the moment, conscious, observing, open for what is new— rather than being a victim of conditioning from the past or of ambitions and expectations for the future.

They can be taken as a prototype which will be validated by doing them and observing or exploring their effects for oneself. As in all growing processes, there is no obvious process as to how the activity produces the faculty. Growing goes through an invisible night process, based on the day activity. The effort in this unusual activity has an effect in the night during sleep when our organism absorbs what we have done in the day and transforms it into capacities or faculties. It may happen that some faculties have been already developed through destiny, or through work, or other schooling. Look at your life story and how it prepared you!

You create the special encounter sphere for spiritual

investigation, with heightened consciousness, able to hold yourself in balance, attuned and transparent as a research instrument. Being wakeful and present, centred in your ego-spirit nature, you are able to move freely in different threshold situations.

## The words, the movement and their synthesis

The exercises combine meditative words for each research step, and hand movements which accompany them (the same basic movement is used each time but naturally varies with the words). The combination of words and movement integrates the forces of thinking, feeling and willing—of meaning and understanding, feeling-sensing, and will engagement—involving the total being. The combination is especially important by bringing the ego into the will sphere.

There are eight exercises, a first general one and seven in sequence for each of the research steps. Each exercise is done in three stages (see diagrams).

1. Observing the polarity and form. Making an outside connection to the polarity, keeping separate the right and left poles.
2. Internalizing the form. Moving the two poles and allowing them to meet within yourself, experiencing it inwardly and centring in yourself.
3. Movement and words come into dynamic objective relation, with you as instrument for it. You create an energy in the open centre.

You are active in another kind of space, beyond the usual, as a first encounter with the spirit in the human being.

## How to do it

The diagrams indicate hand movements, beginning with the left side, then with the right side, with a pause in the centre point. The gestures accompany the meditative words and they are done together. (It is helpful to lay the drawing in front of you.) It is effective to practise each exercise three times successively, which gives an increase in awareness of what is living in the space. After each one it is recommended that you pause to observe the space within you and around you. What is arising in your consciousness? The experiences may also differ each time you do the exercises.

At first the emphasis may be on the words. They should be precisely and exactly experienced and spoken in a concentrated manner. To begin with one can only think the words, then the words are experienced more and more inwardly. At the end the words should be penetrated by our will as if at this moment that which the words express in fact happens. In this way the exercise becomes a will-schooling exercise. It is also helpful to become familiar beforehand with the hand movements so that the concentration is not disturbed in making the synthesis of word and movement.

## The principles and archetypes

You could say this is done on the level of life itself, on the threshold of form and movement, on the interplay of earthly and etheric forces.

The first principle is taken from the archetypal structure of the human being as threefold: standing upright in the centre between right/left, forward/back, above/below. Our universe is built on dualities—day/night, light/dark, heaven/earth, etc. The duality becomes a polarity in the human sphere where a middle space lives in between and can relate to the two poles. The human being can consciously transform the warring tendency of dualities to a harmonizing via the interval between.

Experience has shown that if done with all three forces together—head, heart and hand—the combination brings a deep, existential quality that is placed into the heart sphere in the centre. The integration also helps to prevent flying out at the threshold into thought associations or emotional reactions. The held open space created at the centre of the movement brings together what streams into the consciousness from above down and from below upwards, holding this in the open middle.

The forms take up the vortex principle, which is an archetype in our universe (mysterious forces, spiralling inwards and outwards or upwards and downwards). It connects us to the time stream of past/future, with the interval of the present in a conscious change of direction.

Integration and synthesis is a necessary quality of research forces, rather than analytical breaking down. The effort of integrating and observation of the hindrances that may arise is also part of the schooling. Most important is not what you do but the way of doing it. For instance, your sense of truth now belongs to the whole being, not only for truth in the thought sphere but also knowing in all spheres. The moral dimension appears in the open space as after-effect.

# GENERAL SPIRITUAL RESEARCH FACULTY

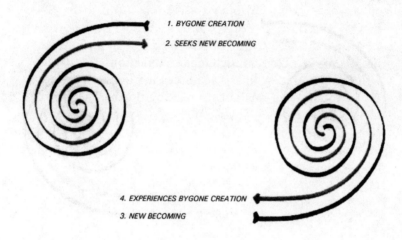

1. BYGONE CREATION
2. SEEKS NEW BECOMING
4. EXPERIENCES BYGONE CREATION
3. NEW BECOMING

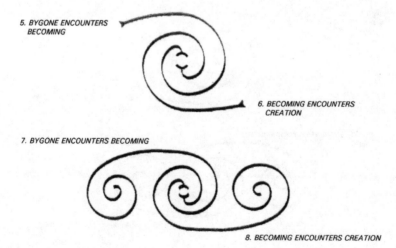

5. BYGONE ENCOUNTERS BECOMING
6. BECOMING ENCOUNTERS CREATION
7. BYGONE ENCOUNTERS BECOMING
8. BECOMING ENCOUNTERS CREATION

# STEP 1: ENCOUNTERING THE RESEARCH QUESTION

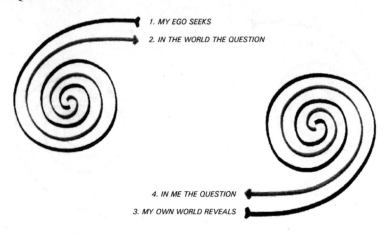

1. MY EGO SEEKS

2. IN THE WORLD THE QUESTION

4. IN ME THE QUESTION

3. MY OWN WORLD REVEALS

5. MY EGO ENCOUNTERS THE ENVIRONMENT

6. THE ENVIRONMENT ENCOUNTERS ME

7. MY EGO ENCOUNTERS MY ENVIRONMENT

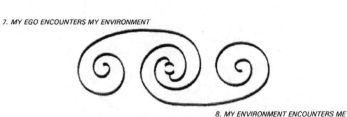

8. MY ENVIRONMENT ENCOUNTERS ME

# STEP 2: BECOMING THE RESEARCH INSTRUMENT

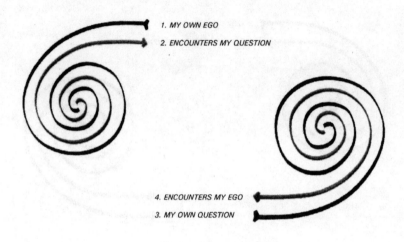

1. MY OWN EGO
2. ENCOUNTERS MY QUESTION
4. ENCOUNTERS MY EGO
3. MY OWN QUESTION

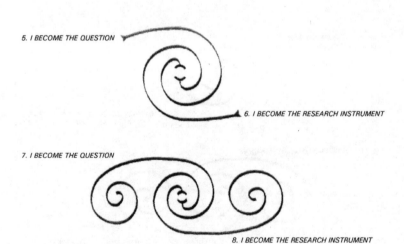

5. I BECOME THE QUESTION
6. I BECOME THE RESEARCH INSTRUMENT
7. I BECOME THE QUESTION
8. I BECOME THE RESEARCH INSTRUMENT

# STEP 3: TRANSFORMING RESISTANCES

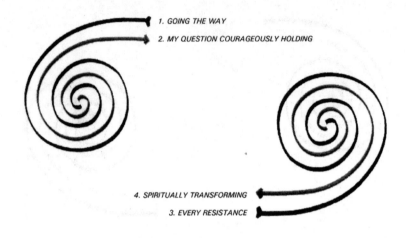

1. GOING THE WAY

2. MY QUESTION COURAGEOUSLY HOLDING

4. SPIRITUALLY TRANSFORMING

3. EVERY RESISTANCE

5. MY STEPS ENCOUNTER MY RESISTANCES

6. MY TRANSFORMED RESISTANCES ENLIGHTEN MY STEPS

7. MY STEPS ENCOUNTER MY RESISTANCES

8. MY TRANSFORMED RESISTANCES ENLIGHTEN MY STEPS

## STEP 4: THRESHOLD BREAKTHROUGH

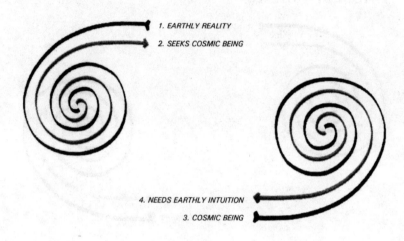

1. EARTHLY REALITY
2. SEEKS COSMIC BEING
4. NEEDS EARTHLY INTUITION
3. COSMIC BEING

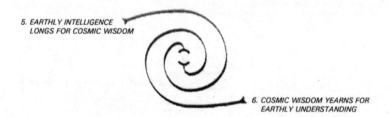

5. EARTHLY INTELLIGENCE
   LONGS FOR COSMIC WISDOM

6. COSMIC WISDOM YEARNS FOR
   EARTHLY UNDERSTANDING

7. EARTHLY INTELLIGENCE ENCOUNTERS COSMIC WISDOM

8. COSMIC WISDOM ENCOUNTERS EARTHLY UNDERSTANDING

## STEP 5: TRANSLATING FOR HUMAN UNDERSTANDING

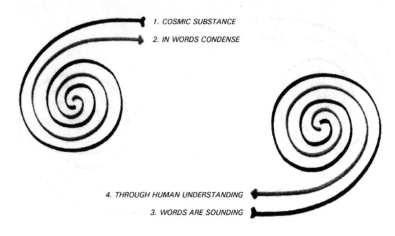

1. COSMIC SUBSTANCE
2. IN WORDS CONDENSE
4. THROUGH HUMAN UNDERSTANDING
3. WORDS ARE SOUNDING

5. SPEAK COSMIC ESSENCE IN HUMAN LANGUAGE
6. THROUGH HUMAN UNDERSTANDING HEAR THE WORD

7. SPEAK COSMIC ESSENCE IN HUMAN LANGUAGE

8. THROUGH HUMAN UNDERSTANDING HEAR THE WORD

# STEP 6: TESTING AND VALIDATING

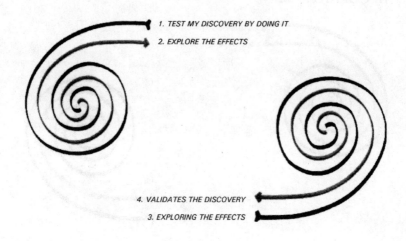

1. TEST MY DISCOVERY BY DOING IT
2. EXPLORE THE EFFECTS

4. VALIDATES THE DISCOVERY
3. EXPLORING THE EFFECTS

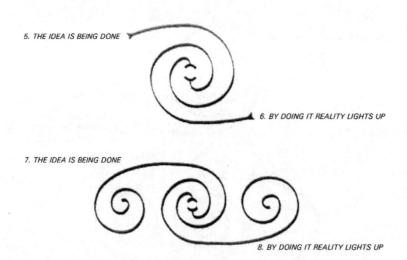

5. THE IDEA IS BEING DONE

6. BY DOING IT REALITY LIGHTS UP

7. THE IDEA IS BEING DONE

8. BY DOING IT REALITY LIGHTS UP

## STEP 7: REALIZATION, FORMING, LETTING GO, BECOMING ANEW

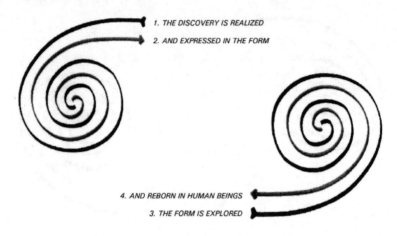

1. THE DISCOVERY IS REALIZED

2. AND EXPRESSED IN THE FORM

4. AND REBORN IN HUMAN BEINGS

3. THE FORM IS EXPLORED

5. IT DIES FROM BEYOND

6. IT IS BORN IN THIS WORLD

7. IT DIES FROM BEYOND

8. IT EXISTS IN THIS WORLD

# 5. Corruption of the Life Processes in Creative Spiritual Research

by Shirley van Houten-Routledge

*This chapter was written out of research and in dialogue with Coenraad van Houten*

The research path goes hand in hand with the inner path of development. In both cases one encounters hindrances, blockages, and resistances. This belongs to the modern initiation way. They have the purpose of developing the forces and faculties we need to go further. When we take them on and transform them, our research instrument is made ready and the open space is prepared for the 'breakthrough', for the new discoveries.

These hindrances may be related to our own personal development path or to our karmic past, or the hindrances may pertain to the particular nature of the research question. Each research field will present certain kinds of hindrances.

There is, however, another level of hindrances, which is archetypal and part of our evolutionary development, and it relates to the basic seven life processes. The life processes are a natural force in our etheric organism. As we use them more consciously and move towards spiritual thresholds, we meet also the 'corruption' of these forces—what happens when they are used to excess, or misused. The 'corruptions' are extreme in our time, further challenging us to develop our individual spirit ground.

The corruption today means the processes are too deeply bound to the physical process and lose connection with their spiritual sources.

Thus it is important to be aware how we meet them and how we can heal them with schooling exercises. Rudolf Steiner briefly named them as follows in *The Riddle of Humanity* (lecture of 3 September 1916, Dornach GA 170).

Here we will give some examples of how they manifest in practice.

| Life process | Corruption |
| --- | --- |
| 1. Breathing | Consumption, using up |
| 2. Warming | Combustion, burning up |
| 3. Nourishing | Hoarding, depositing |
| 4. Individualizing is free of the corrupting forces | |
| 5. Maintaining | Sclerosis, hardening |
| 6. Growing | Premature ripening, maturing |
| 7. Reproducing | Regeneration, procreation, repetition |

As described in Steiner's spiritual science: in the creating of our human being, the highest creative powers instilled the possibility of failure so that the human creature could become a free spirit. For this they arranged a positive deliberate corruption of our life processes by allowing two great powers to take on a task. These two great powers Steiner called Lucifer and Ahriman. We can know them in their corruption, when they press their task too deeply into the physical realm. They then become an evil force as an excessive power in us.

The luciferic forces have the task to generate the greatest possible self-consciousness, giving us an inner, subjective truth. This power is not concerned about an objective truth, but wants only to expand our consciousness too soon with self-gratification and passion. False interpretations usually take over and blind the common sense.

Ahrimanic forces have the task to put our energies into matter, into physical effects, without concern for objective truth or moral purpose. This power would condense and harden into physical certainty with pragmatic quick solutions, with no space for the paradigm shift, and is only interested for the effect of an idea and how it can be used. It likes to fix memories and facts into convenient systems.

Thus there is luciferic corruption in the direction of an illusionary consciousness, and ahrimanic in the direction of lying and falsehood. The first three life processes are under the influence of Ahriman, the last three that of Lucifer. In the middle is an open space, untouchable.

Steiner wrote extensively about the nature of these two powers and how they reinforce each other. Here only one aspect is mentioned that is relevant to the research theme. This spiritual background you may accept or not, but the phenomena are real and ask for our awareness. Our task then is to learn to observe and investigate, objectively, selflessly.

R. Steiner, in the lecture mentioned above, states:

> The aberrations must be possible, as otherwise a human being could not determine his path in the cosmos through the use of his own free will. Finding the right path for our development depends precisely upon learning to maintain our sovereignty against the ahrimanic and luciferic influences. It depends on constant struggle to maintain our balance between these two powers, so it is inevitable that the things that only the power of Lucifer and Ahriman can give us, also make it possible for us to go astray.

## Some examples of corruption

The following are a few examples of corruptions. However, they may take on many different forms and need to be researched, each for oneself.

### 1. Breathing, corruption to consumption

Breathing in the body takes in oxygen and gives out carbon dioxide, a polluting substance. Within us something happens to the purity of that which we take in; we change it and use it up. The breathing process on the etheric level, as life process, is a breathing through the senses. And what do we do with what we thus absorb and breathe out?

Our modern state of consciousness makes all we perceive into things, facts, concepts, mental pictures—in other words, we stay on the physical surfaces and do not 'see' the forces and worlds behind the outer appearances. Our inner sense-stimulated movement, or judgement process, can misinterpret what we outwardly experience. This is a corruption of the breathing process. However, the sensing process gives us a strong experience of being an independent self.

Our modern lifestyle offers a bombardment of the senses, giving a lustful joy for endless new experiences. We use up our intelligence with sense-bound activities in a superficial, materialistic way, living on the surfaces and in the world of things. By this we can strongly experience our self, but we also become more mortal and earthbound. We breathe in something alive and kill it inwardly by fixing into concepts, information or abstract knowledge. This gives us certainty in the material world. If we live within this boundary, however, with no sense for the life processes within this material world and covering it up with our mental pictures, then we can find no confidence that there is a spiritual reality.

In learning, for example, we may gather up information, curious to know more and more, but are not able to digest or breathe out or put into practice. We consume and become a highly intelligent information source, seemingly wise but superficial in substance and empty of life. What is then 'real'?

We may encounter at the threshold the phenomena of the mirror, not realizing what we 'see' outwardly is a projection of what is within the self. Or we are not aware of the invisible glass which is reflecting the phenomenon in us.

Are we aware what is happening within us as the breathing process? Where is the borderline of earthly and spiritual and can we learn to perceive in both worlds?

## 2. Warming, corruption to combustion

Warmth has to do with our life forces, the secret of life itself. We long to experience life. What is 'life'? Warmth is the invisible bridging medium between earthly and spiritual worlds.

One way to observe this process is to ask what uses up energy and what gives energy. Usually we use up life forces, consume our organism, often for the wrong reasons.

The speed of change is, for instance, too fast for a healthy evolution. We can move speedily with fiery enthusiasm, no longer observe what is happening in the moment, and want to get to the future immediately.

If energy is directed only to earthly activity, our life forces are used up, burned up, not replenished, and we end up in 'burn out'—a common modern ailment. Or in thinking we use only the reflection activity of the brain, abstractions not warmed through with understanding or a living human activity. This manifests in the phenomena of cynicism, abstraction, mechanical thinking—the spiritual content of words dies, is extinguished to lifeless ashes. If we try to force a situation, are too ambitious or hasty, don't let warming processes show where the life is, we burn it up and lose the living quality.

## 3. Nourishing, corruption to hoarding
Learning systems fill us up with material, 'foreign matter', which we need to digest in order to make usable. Does the knowledge feed and nourish, or is one only hoarding it? Some people are skilled in an encyclopedic gathering of knowledge, can quote who said what, when and where, but are only able to quote it, not use it.

Just as the body stores up fat from matter that cannot be transformed, we can accumulate and build up an inner library, create our own universe, more and more separated from the world, wrapped up in self. We measure the world against our own standards and educated expectations. A related tendency is to 'research' by combining things that should not be combined, reading, combining, associating one field to another. We can build up a make-believe world, which we believe is real because we are in it. When we have a question before us, we may gather old experiences out of our inner library to put onto the question, and perhaps have not really heard the question! Hoarding means living in the past.

Another common distortion is reducing spiritual research to technical information, which cannot explain the real phenomena; the computer logic of this world is applied to spiritual material. But the spiritual cannot be recorded by technology!

Hence we need a new kind of knowing. Normal knowledge lives on the surfaces, on the boundary to the spiritual world but not within it. Corruption means staying on the physical side. A new knowing will be more active, intensive, involved in what lives in the beingness itself and within world processes.

## 4. Individualizing

In the book *The Riddle of Humanity* Rudolf Steiner briefly indicated the corruption of the life processes, but he did not elaborate or explain further. Why did he indicate that the fourth life process was not accessible to these corrupting forces? He left us with this mystery to explore. In practice, doing the creative research process, it became clear: there is an open space within us wherein we can experience the total otherness of spiritual realities. We call it crossing the threshold. Many authors and seers write or teach about this. For instance Eckhart Tolle speaks of 'the power of now', Otto Scharmer speaks of 'presence', Joseph Beuys speaks of the nothingness out of which real creativity comes and wherein the call of the future may be heard.

With our present evolved consciousness most people have glimpses of this; it requires an active inner effort and uprightness to open our soul-spirit for it. Therefore the exercises were developed as in the next chapter of this book, to create the open middle space. It requires other centring and balancing forces and conscious presence for the threshold encounter.

## 5. Maintaining, corruption to hardening

Longing for certainty, we hold fast to what we know, fix it into a form and keep it that way. In step 4 something was discovered, but it is not yet filled. If fixed into words too soon, the movement stops and does not reach deeper levels. Maintaining should be a process with continuity, not information gathering.

We may identify with our experience, deeply impressed by the spiritual moment, and live in the memory. We can even fall in love with what we have found—don't need to go any further. Or we form conclusions or interpretations too quickly, not working our insights through enough that others can understand. Fixations of roles, lifestyles, what we know that we know, convictions, patterns learned in the past, can impose themselves on understanding the new discovery. Further development is hindered by a feeling of being already at our goal and perfect enough. One may lose contact with the whole, with the context of the discovery and become one-sided. It takes on a life of its own.

## 6. Growing, corruption to premature ripening

In nature we know that growing is a process in time, with phases of growth and decay, of overripeness or under-ripeness, within influences from the environment.

Growing for research has to do with being ready to apply a new insight in practice in life. When is the right time? Is it too soon, and will it wither or fade away because there is not enough substance in it? Is it mature enough, spiritually sub-stantial enough? Is the environment well enough prepared for it? If too quickly applied it may be consumed as in step 2, rather than growing stronger as in step 6. Because we are so convinced of the rightness and importance of what we have discovered, we fail to test it sufficiently; then act as if it is ready and real, perhaps imposing on the environment some-thing that is underripe or unsuitable. Have we listened to the environment and know by intuition what is possible in the present moment? On the other hand, are we too hesitant, wanting to be too perfect, and are thus too late?

When this process is not spiritualized, and our egocentric day consciousness assumes the creation of the course of our life, this force is applied only to a strong aspiration for achievement. It mutates then to the aspiration to achieve success in life at all costs, to feel happy on the soul level and be personally admired. This wish becomes then the all-embracing life aim. What nature has wisely given to us is thereby misused and becomes a force which makes the 'aspiration to achieve' the aim of life, and an organic growing process instead becomes an 'all-consuming ambition'. In other words, 'ripening' here is not a natural organic process but an artificial, cultivated aspiration to harvest more and different substance from what has originally been sown—an overbreeding and exaggeration, corrupting the healthy life process. This ambition is the strongest blockage for research step 6. The often heard sentence 'It works, it functions, so it must be right' is an expression of this interfering ambition which becomes a habitual pragmatic blockage. A great help here to make the new idea earth-ripe would be to understand that our destiny is created out of many biographies—at least the last life, the life between death and a new birth, and the present biography.

Application in life requires also being ready to identify with and give one's own life forces to bring the insight alive in the world, not only within oneself. We can be now consumed with pride of accomplishment—how brilliant; what genius! Atom-smashing machines, nuclear fusions, genetic engineering etc. can be done—but why do this? What intention or moral motivation is behind it?

### 7. Reproducing, corruption to repetition
This is a reflection of the first step of breathing, taking in and giving out. Is there anything new as culmination, or just adjusting or repeating what was already there with a new variation? If the research is not finished, a real reproduction process is prevented—it may be just fixed into a new type or a patented piece. Now it is a question of whether the new is so specialized as to be out of context with the whole, either in the physical sense or the spiritual context. Does it serve humanity, or only a particular sect?

Reproduction as we have known it involves bringing together two one-sided entities (such as male and female) which by joining together can make the new; they give rise to another physical entity. Towards the future reproduction, the aim will be a new kind of coming together of two or more to co-create what one alone cannot do—spiritually co-creating, co-working, not only physically procreating or regenerating.

Hence the question arises: Does the creative person now hang onto their new insight, possess it, keep repeating it, identify with it, or are they able to give it out for others to take up and become newly creative with it? It becomes clear in this process to what extent the individualizing has taken place in the centre, in the fourth life process, and how much has been spirit-filled and selflessly concerned for humanity, and in harmony with cosmic realities.

# Part Two: Aspects of Self-development and Transformation

The following chapters are on aspects of the general spiritual schooling that apply to self-development and transformation, and are therefore not only for support of spiritual research and spiritual creativity.

For many people it takes considerable courage to come to a research question. Our present culture and education does not support this way—it offers an answer culture, not a question culture!

Each individual must find his/her own spiritual path and sort through the wide expanse of supersensible methods becoming available. Therefore the most crucial faculty to be schooled is *individual discernment*—being able to look through and correctly evaluate what one meets or experiences.

On the research path there will be blockages or diversions to be overcome for which these schooling exercises will be helpful.

# 6. Schooling Observation and Independent Judgement

by Shirley van Houten-Routledge

## Part 1: Where we are starting from. The given situation

As a human being we live in a functioning organism within a boundary encircled by 12 senses. These 12 senses are given in the human design to make it possible to exist in the physical world. They are as 12 windows, giving 12 kinds of experience of self and world. We are constantly breathing between inner self and outer world through this sensing instrument.

Thanks to this twelvefold organism we can develop an independent intelligence. We can develop the faculty to distinguish what is what and what is happening to me. However, this functioning is still bound to the earthly experience in a body, and to a sense-bound intelligence.

Through sensory experience we build up over the years an inner library of learning and experience. We can say 'I know what I know'. With this we can indulge in the 'thing-filled' world; when we relate self to images and impressions, grounded in a sense-stimulated applied intelligence, we gain a certain kind of reality and certainty.

As we search deeper to understand ourselves, we come to a boundary—a boundary where all the knowledge gained from the sense-perceptible world ends and our deeper questions of meaning and understanding can go no further. The material world gives no answers; it shows us pictures, images, things— a semblance of reality. These perceptions, however, are an outer expression of their inner secrets. Thanks to our emerging consciousness soul condition, we can now begin to discern what is behind the sense appearance, what streams through us, previously without our conscious awareness. Thus we stand on this boundary or threshold of consciousness.

The present epoch of time is offering this as our development task, to evolve new human faculties. This essay describes one part of the schooling path which empowers this human creative potential. We can call this *the schooling of observation and independent judgement.*

*The very first step is to choose, to want to take it on, and to make an inner shift from passive to active.*

## The schooling of observation

Every new sense stimulus we receive we must connect to our inner library as a first action. The human soul must maintain its wholeness in this way. The sense perception stirs an inner movement and a reaction or response comes up within, which we usually send out again into the environment. The reaction or response includes a wide range of possibilities and is quite unique to each individual. These are not typical behaviour patterns as humanistic psychology would like to suggest. This only applies in so far as you look at built-in functions or animal-like instincts for survival. A human being has other layers out of which the inner reaction can be stirred, including educated patterns and the individual pre-birth preparation and karmic constitution. So long as these are not consciously penetrated all the levels function like an instinct and are rather automatic.

The schooling of observation means becoming aware of the 'inner library' and being able to withhold that, to see more clearly. It is not easy to do because so much certainty is attached to our identification with our inner library of knowledge. We may find an attachment to our models, mental constructs, sufferings, roles and functions, the way we have adjusted to the world, how we are conditioned and educated, what we believe we know, etc. To create an open not-knowing space may cause fear. But only then can the hidden side show itself to us. Hence we need a secure process to develop another kind of certainty.

*Experiment:* Try an exercise in observing. Place an object in the centre of the group, covered over so it is not visible (or ask people to close their eyes); then remove the cover for 3–4 seconds, let everyone look at it, then cover it again. Now each person looks within to observe what was going on during those 3-4 seconds. When they share, each person can make the discovery of how much is happening very rapidly. Try to stretch out those few seconds and observe your own steps. For instance—

- Perhaps there was an instantaneous recognition and a naming of the object. However this must have been preceded by a number of observations, also connecting to previous experiences, as well as an inner question 'What is it?'
- The perception may send one on an inner journey through memories, associations, sympathies or antipathies, pre-conceived judgements, inner convictions, wishes, desires, drives, impulses, etc. etc.

The reality is, that this initial response tells you about your own soul world and your relationship to the outer thing. It may or may not tell you about the object itself. You remain tied to the past, hindering motivation to the future.

Therefore the first step of schooling in observation is to become aware of one's own reactive constitution. We have it. We need it. But we need to go further to understand the world or the other person.

If we stay within our body-bound sense organism with its instinctive wisdom, emotions and drives, if the ego is caught in its body-consciousness, one can eventually lose faith in life. It becomes empty of meaning and depressions will be inevitable. Then the spirit dimension, which the soul longs for and which is the other part of reality, has been denied. From the body-bound level of intelligence and emotion, solutions to world needs or human problems of today will not be found. Our questions will meet a boundary of darkness.

In short, the 12 senses can be earthbound, perceiving the 'semblance' realm: 'I see the world around me; my senses serve me'. Or our attention can be directed also to higher levels; the 12 senses become *windows* through which reality speaks to you. A new spiritual science is needed to explore the invisible dimension of our reality, for instance to read the meaning in the phenomena. For spiritual research *the human being itself is the instrument.* The upright human being stands between, mediates between earthly and spiritual realms. Therefore the human ego must become aware of itself as a research instrument, and fine tune its functioning, *building a bridge between the two worlds.*

The basic first exercise in schooling observation faculties starts as in the exercise above:

1. Observe outwardly an object, using your senses.
2. Observe inwardly your reactive stirrings.

Then it goes on:

3. Acknowledge and suspend your own inner busyness. Objectively observe the object as it is in itself. (It helps if you can come to an inner stillness, so that the object has an undisturbed mirror in you to show itself. Your inner attitude of open interest will also determine what you are able or permitted to see.)
4. Notice inwardly what effect step 3 has had on you, and how your relationship to the object changes, and what attitude you are left with.

Each of these steps can be shared in a group of three or more people. You may find in doing the exercise that your interest is awakened, or a mood of wonder arises, or your energy is more alive. To *awaken interest* in a world that has become boring is one of the aims of this first stage.

The third step above can be ever more enhanced by the questions you put before your eyes. You may for instance devise a process of observing the same object over a number of days:

1. Observe the physical facts.
2. Observe their relationships and patterns of forms, life conditions.

3. Observe the qualities, gesture towards environment.
4. Observe ideas, intelligence incorporated into its composition or design.
5. Observe its statement and place in the universe; its purpose to be.

As you experiment with these ways of observing, you may discover each asks for a different kind of activity in yourself. Observe yourself observing and, if practising in a group, share what kind of inner activity you experienced. Help one another discern when are you busy with your self and your own library of knowledge, and when are you engaged with the object itself.

This activity awakens your ego-centre as the director of your percept-concept processes (which has a different inner level than stimulus-response mechanisms). Then the 'observer consciousness' is given its true place. In addition the ego-centre can learn to observe your inner world objectively as if it is an outer world. You can then observe yourself observing, and how you come to your conclusions or decisions. In other words, *we first awaken to our ego-centre, our I-ness, then secondly to knowing what and how we are observing while we are observing.*

In today's world this schooling is very necessary as we are subjected to excessive sense-bombardment and stimulation. It is important to create *an open space* in the sensing process, so the human being can be present, conscious, and freely choosing how to participate, replacing the reactive with one's own independent activity.

With this preparation we can move to the next stage.

## Part 2: Passive to active schooling path

As our observer nature matures and becomes more finely tuned, we develop a sense organ for every level of experience. The 12 given senses can be enhanced to deeper levels of perception. The soul forces of thinking, feeling and willing can *also* become organs of perception for soul and spirit dimensions.

The schooling begins with the inner shift already indicated—the shift from passive to active! The development potential has been given to us. But the darkness experience of the sense world stays unless we freely choose to be an active participant in this development. The next step is to be active in three ways in observation:

- Attentiveness
- Devotion or empathy
- Uprightness

These are three different activities, the third arising out of practising the other two. Your 'I'—your ego centre—directs your activity. You create an open space in yourself to be active in between the sense perceptions and inner reactions, replacing your automatic responses with conscious sensing, discerning and deciding.

With *attentiveness* we direct ourselves outwards and move towards the world to discover as much as possible through our senses about the object one is focused upon. We step outside our habitual ways of looking to openly observe without making any conclusions.

*Empathy or devotion* is an opposite gesture, opening myself in a listening-receiving mode, allowing the object to impress itself in me. I experience its nature, tone, quality, as best I can, reading the impression it makes.

With this activity, it is especially important to be able to discern the different feelings we experience, for instance what effect the object has on me and how I feel about it versus a feeling for the object in its nature. We can encounter the deeper truth of the object when part of our soul forces have been transformed to organs of perception—

- Our thinking becomes like a touching
- Our feeling becomes experiencing the tone or quality, how it is to be in the state of existence of otherness
- Our willing becomes a knowing

'Knowing' is not only a cognitive activity. We can also develop a feeling-knowing (heart sensing) and a willing-knowing (for beingness of the other). We learn also to discern when we are using our sense of thought to grasp the idea or concept, and when we actually begin to think as an activity.

When we know ourselves well enough, we are able to become one with the beingness or reality of the 'other' without losing our own centre of consciousness. We are fully present as an individual ego being, but selfless at the same time. We keep our individual *uprightness* wherever we move and whatever assails us, and are not taken over by new impressions. Then the willing-knowing-intuition faculty awakens. We can experience the being or life quality of what we are observing, seeing more than we see. This is one example of a threshold crossing, through the senses to the being behind the outer appearances.

Most observation training, as in science or even Goethean observation, emphasizes the attentiveness and how we are informed by this activity. However, less emphasis has been given on the 'empathy' or 'listening-into' activity. There is an open field here to develop exercises for schooling this, as well as bringing all three together—attentiveness, devotion and uprightness. This does not happen automatically, just by wanting it, but by an inner effort of self-transformation and development.

*Exercise examples:* To practise these activities, you can follow the same exercises as before, but make a conscious change from being outwardly attentive in order to get to know the object as well as possible to then shifting to the opposite gesture. Openly receive and listen into the object and notice how it resonates within, then tell one another how it speaks to you about itself.

The following is a sample exercise that focuses only on the second activity of devotion.

Form in groups of 4–5 people. Steps 1 and 2 of the exercise are done with the eyes closed.

1. Each group is given an object. This is passed from person to person. Each tries to sense the qualities of the object. Attune yourself to it; let it resound in you. (Naming it might happen but is not necessary for the exercise.)
2. In inner quiet translate your experience of the object to 3 or 4 sounds that express its qualities (not a word, just vowels, consonants, tones, sounds).
3. Objects are removed. Eyes can be opened. Share with the group your sounds. Listen to each other. Arrange the 4 or 5 sounds into a sequence and sound one after another. Share your group composition with other groups.
4. Review process. What discoveries and experiences were unusual? Where was your attention focused, and how did it move? (Note: objects may be different per group, such as rock, crystal, shell, feather, large leaf, etc.)
5. Bring objects back and look at them. What discoveries arise about the way of observing without using sight?

The three activities—attentiveness, empathy, upright-ness—prepare for a consciousness that is not body-bound but eventually will be able to *perceive on other levels of reality*, moving between physical and supersensible worlds without losing one's centre of awareness and balance. The modern spiritual scientist stays upright and present, aware of the spiritual world within the sense world and therefore able to integrate spiritual realities with daily living. This way of perceiving is a new kind of 'clairvoyance' that comes with understanding and an individualized spirit-knowing.

This path *through the senses to the spirit* is described by Rudolf Steiner who called it a new yoga—yoga of light. We breathe in light through our senses experience. There flows within this breathing not only the images and outer appear-ances, but also an invisible spiritual stream. Our mission today is to reconnect with our divine origins via this activity.

It begins with our active participation, which through our *interest* creates a medium of warmth between self and world, a newly created warmth substance. Warmth is a mediating medium which penetrates both physical and spiritual realms and makes possible the streaming of light. Therefore our inner attitude is important as we approach what we want to observe.

The expansion of our sensing faculties is growing through the night during sleep, according to how we have been active in the day in our sensing activity. How have we filled this activity with consciousness, in thinking, in speaking and listening, and in doing?

This Part 2 of Schooling Observation has the aim of developing our soul instrument to become transparent and available, to perceive the world as an outer manifestation of the invisible reality. The path could be described as a development from—

- Instinctual consciousness
- Day consciousness separating outer and inner worlds
- Active presence in between
- Higher consciousness, unifying material and spiritual worlds

The way of working here outlined for observation and discernment has the ultimate aim to integrate the spiritual dimension into daily life. Before we reach that ultimate goal, however, the way of working and the inner attitude shifts already change our experiences and understanding of what we meet in daily life. Thus the schooling of observation is not only to be a more effective observer, but is also an inner development of faculties, attitudes, and levels of awareness.

## Part 3: Independent judgement or discernment

The other side of observation is that we should arrive at some action, whether cognitive recognition, aesthetic sense for what the situation is at this moment, or a deed that will be morally fruitful. This is often called forming 'independent judgements'. The sense perception has stirred an inner movement, which will find some kind of conclusion. There can be no *real* judgement unless we have first really observed.

It is crucial to investigate our judgement-forming process because our judgements have consequences vital for research and also affect every aspect of work, social relationships, and daily life—how we understand or misunderstand. When approaching spiritual thresholds and spiritual research, another field opens up for observation, where judgement processes also change.

## Reactive level
As described in 'The schooling of observation' (p. 92), in the first instance we meet our 'reactive' person, our inner library or self-enclosed universe. Throughout our life so far we have accumulated learning and knowledge, influences, experiences, heritage, traditions, conditioning, memories, etc., creating our own world which enables us to function in life and be competent in our way of handling it. Most of our judgement processes happen on this level.

Behind the 'reactive' person is a deeper level of sources out of the karmic past, for which our reactions can give signals—especially when very strong feelings, convictions, or impulses arise, not rational or explainable in the situation. Thus the destiny learning path also requires a new opening for discerning the meaning behind human phenomena.

## Phenomenology level
Another way of forming judgements comes from the phenomenology approach, such as Goethe developed it, to hold back judgements out of oneself and allow the truth of what lives in the phenomena to speak itself to you. This needs a deeper listening faculty, withholding the need for immediate answers, slowing down the usual reactive judgement process. The initial thinking conclusions will be there, also being busy with our feeling and impulses, but this is acknowledged and set aside to allow an open space, a still space into which another truth can show itself. This process can be supported by taking the open space into the night, with an open question, and examine the result the next day.

## Open space

We can already realize that the kind of question we ask and the attitude we hold inwardly will affect what we perceive and how we understand it. Most essential is to be aware of the space between self and world—how our ego is active and present in this encounter area. A very different conclusion will arise if we impose our self onto the environment, or if we withhold our self to listen to what speaks from the environment. The first gesture will perpetuate the past; the second will allow the future or the new vision to shine through.

## Independence

As the ego becomes active and more conscious in this process, there comes to consciousness a deep *urge for independence*, the urge to be my true self, free from ... free from what? The individualizing of the human spirit is our present evolutionary step. We meet this in every judgement process, every decision, as an opportunity to exercise creating a 'free space'. Am I holding onto security of past learning and traditions, customs, systems, etc.? Is my judgement 'independent' in the present, versus driven by past or future influences? How clear and unbiased are we? At the same time we must stand upon our present foundations of knowledge and understanding— we cannot do otherwise—but be always open for new or deeper insight. As we achieve an open space consciousness, we can also experience freedom as such, not just 'freedom from'. *A new creativity space arises.*

For research, the level of judgements concerns the spiritual dimension. As new eyes are opening, this affects the way of handling social life, in relationships, karmic perception, spirituality in people, responsibilities, capacities, differences and most essential, the deeds we do or do not do. Our 'independent' judgements have consequences not only for oneself, but are also existential for others and for our environment.

The familiar tendency in social situations is to justify oneself. Each person digs up their knowledge and intelligence to apply and then to convince others of its validity—in other words, calling on our inner library. Even spiritual knowledge can be heavy ammunition to justify one's views, especially when it becomes dogmatic, fanatical or fundamentalist. Now the moral dimension and awareness of consequences becomes essential. We meet special challenges, such as:

- Can we sense and respect the spiritual stature of another? How authentic is their 'authority' on spiritual matters? Do we have confidence in our own authenticity?
- Can I make my own true judgement? Can I trust my own judgements?
- Can we recognize a fellow being in their true being, their karmic context, their capabilities and potential?
- Can we recognize a paradigm shift, or new breakthrough, or validity of a new discovery?
- How do we recognize what is old or new clairvoyance? How can we understand our threshold experiences?

It takes courage to make one's own judgement, and courage also to let go of a fixed judgement.

### Processes of schooling judgement faculties

While we are engaged in *consciousness* within the sense organism, we experience observation and judgement as separate, as an outer and an inner activity. When however the *ego* becomes supersensibly active, there is no separation—the outer and inner are united. For instance, we perceive outwardly and know the inner meaning at the same time. It is necessary, however, to strengthen the ego forces first so that we are able to move in both realms and keep our consciousness, discernment and sanity.

Because of the present expansion of consciousness, pressing beyond the boundaries of the sense world, our inner activities of thinking, feeling and willing are separating, each taking on a life of its own. Therefore also our capacity for clear judgements is fragmenting. (See Chapter 7, 'Thresholds of Consciousness'.)

The central point is *consciousness*; the path begins with the ego being self-conscious and builds from there to expanding levels of awareness. Part of our schooling therefore will be learning to discern what is the nature of this threshold and where the boundary of the sense world is, also closely observing our own judgement processes.

## Truth, beauty and goodness

As the human being finds its existence in the *physical* world, we grow into and enter the mineral, plant and animal realms. Through the senses we live and find our experience of self. This is the world we experience as our reality. As the human being grows into *spiritual* worlds, he grows into different realms of experience where earthly logic no longer applies.

Since time immemorial three soul qualities were spoken of as ideals of humanity, indicating a spiritual realm beyond the earthly realm. Truth, beauty and goodness are these ideals coming from beyond the sense boundary and standing as openings to a spiritual life. They are universally human, not exclusive to any special group. In the course of time we have become aware of these three words, which describe a part of our humanness that always remains supersensible. In the deepest inwardness of soul, the human being longs for the spiritual.

Plato spoke of these three, truth, beauty and goodness, and added a fourth quality which he called 'justice', meaning the ability to give our lives direction, to know the self and orient the self in life. We could also use the word 'uprightness' instead of justice.

## Three kinds of judgement forming

We meet the foregoing three ideals now in the form of the three kinds of judgement activity—cognitive judgement, aesthetic judgement and moral judgement. The cognitive judgement is most familiar and most conscious, because we are so strongly focused on intelligence to lead us. Today, in the twenty-first century, however, the moral is becoming ever more conscious and essential. The consciousness soul longs for understanding of the deepest layers of its being and purpose. The individualized ego longs for its own sense of knowing, of goodness and making free choices. Every awakening soul asks 'Who am I really?' and 'What am I here for?'

What used to be unconscious or regulated by social or religious customs is now open to scrutiny and transformation. Humanity is at war with itself, battling to find the real meaning of being human. The aesthetic relation to feeling life is most neglected in our modern education, but can be a key to reconnecting our fragmented nature and to reconnecting spiritual and earthly experiences.

It is worth pointing out that in today's world the necessity of developing independent judgement is acute. The confusion between inner and outer worlds has vastly increased, with accompanying psychological problems. In communications the spreading of disinformation is a new science of manipulating people. It has become highly professional in economics and politics. The media messages are often not believable. Truth, beauty and goodness appear in their opposites, as the lie, the ugly, the immoral or inhuman. These three ideals can be explored through exercises with a Manichaean process, observing phenomena and their opposites. The 'Manichaean' way would be to take these phenomena into oneself, finding one's inner experiences, transforming them inwardly, then we know how to act outwardly. An independent sense of truth, beauty and morality is the only antidote.

So it is ever more necessary to understand how our soul forces function as standing on and crossing over the borderline of the sense and supersensible realms. We can now look at how our three kinds of judgement function.

### Aesthetic judgement

Making 'judgements' begins in the middle, from an awareness in the feeling soul, and moves upwards to the cognitive or downwards to the moral will. The sense of truth is actually a deep, sometimes hidden feeling. Thus we may begin at the middle.

Whereas our thinking judgements and moral judgements are consequential for other people and our environment, the aesthetic judgement has at first consequences only for oneself.

It serves to connect us to the world, and to who we are. Initially therefore it is essential to the development of individualized awareness. Part of the feeling forces can be schooled to become an organ of perception where the aesthetic feeling can be extended to become a social sense organ for the situation (also a karma perception), for what lives as qualities and gestures behind the outer appearances. One becomes an artist of human life, towards a future social art. The artistic sense becomes a social sense, stretching beyond the subjective self.

What is beauty? What is beautiful? An artist making a painting is never satisfied that it is right, and finished. It is always in process. There is no conclusion as in the cognitive understanding or the moral deed. The aesthetic is weaving and moving in the situation, sensing where we are now. It is very inward, involving something to be done within oneself. We are answerable to no one but ourselves in the process. We are constantly in process. As we take this up to consciousness we learn to think in living processes. As we take it towards the moral, we learn situational judgement.

To delve deeply into our humanity we must call on the help of feelings. We need this to live into spiritual realms (truth, beauty and goodness) and also to stay human as we enter the mineral, plant and animal worlds. As we cross thresholds of consciousness into unknown spheres, the upright feeling centre keeps us in balance and aware.

Therefore, in summary, the aesthetic is schooled in artistic exercises or creating a work of art, and then can grow to be a selfless organ for sensing into the situation of another, or into the invisible world behind the sense perceptible and bringing this back into an expression of a truth. The more the art shows the 'truth', the more it is 'beautiful', as a new definition for what beauty is.

Coenraad van Houten describes this judgement process as 'experiencing', an encounter event in the moment, of living between two worlds. It becomes ever more effective as we learn to hold the open space, the interval between outer perception and inner experience.

## Cognitive judgement

The cognitive judgement involves a process of getting to know, understand and recognize the essential nature of an object, of whatever kind. It is strongly connected with sense perceptions and sense stimulus. The object can be either an inner or an outer experience. Anything subjective disturbs and distorts this process, and must therefore be put aside. We are concerned solely with persuading the object itself to reveal what it is really like.

(C. van Houten)

Truth is experienced in the sphere of the mind, using also the medium of the senses of the physical body and the physical world. We experience the physical world as a world of things, of definable objects. Thus we tend to think of truth also as finite things, a truth being complete in itself—'The Truth'. The world of thought and ideas however is not of this nature, but of an etheric force-field, moving, weaving, interpenetrating, integrating, creating.

As we progress in our inner path and become less body-bound, less submerged in the physical realm, we begin to think on an etheric level, where truth is experienced as free impulses, as consequential, a living thinking activity. What any one person is thinking has an effect in the etheric world and therefore on other people. Hence as we become more free and more awake, we also become more responsible, co-responsible, for what flows between the external world and our own inner world. The cosmic world of thought and word is increasingly accessible in so far as our ego is strong enough to care for this awareness.

Truth does not come instantly. It is essential therefore to withhold as long as possible coming to a final conclusion, but look from as many different viewpoints as possible. We tend to want immediate answers, and we want to put them into words immediately. Some try to find the truth by speaking out all the thoughts they hold. This tendency bothers the cognitive judgement process.

Whereas the aesthetic judgement is very much involving my

person, the cognitive sense requires that we put our own person out of the way, and let the thing being observed speak itself to us. Thinking becomes like a touching, rather than 'putting a judgement upon'. The attitude with which we are active will determine what we are allowed to see. The facts are objective in themselves; the sense organs are neutral; our inner activity can be distorting or clearing, finding illusion or truth.

*A small example regarding judgement forming:* I looked out the window and saw a light in the bush outside the house. From past experience and knowledge I know it is impossible that there is a light in the bush. What was I seeing? Then I saw that a lamp inside the house was on. Ah—I am seeing a reflection via the glass in the window. The phenomenon 'light in bush' had its source elsewhere, but the medium that makes it possible to see this was invisible. Then many questions came to mind:

- How often am I seeing mirrored reflections only of a reality from another source? Is the sense world full of reflections, semblance, like a 'house of mirrors'? What is 'real'?
- Why did I not see the reflection in the glass? (There seemed to be a special situation in this case, as if the light was really out there, the glass was invisible.)
- Do I really see what I see?
- Is my self-picture also a mirrored reflection only and not the real self?
- When I look at the world and see a quality I don't like, am I aware of the mirror and perhaps seeing something of my unconscious self reflected? (Psychology calls it projection, etc.)

Where is the border of semblance and reality? What is the invisible glass?

## Moral judgement

Morality is concerned with the relation of the entire human being to the external world—not, however, to the physical

external world, but rather to the spiritual forces and powers
that surround us ... Morality is truly something that works
into humanity directly from the spiritual world.

(Rudolf Steiner)

Moral impulses work directly on the human ego, and therefore can only arise responsibly in a conscious human ego. The
radiating ego has in turn an effect on his spiritual *and* human
environment. The conscious mind is engaged in the process
but as part of the whole organism, not separated as a physical
brain function. The moral impulses come to consciousness by
way of the head, but the essence of the moral is in the will, in
the deeds we do and the attitudes out of which we act.

The moral judgement capacity is relatively new in human
development as an inner individualized function, and less and
less regulated by outer rules and traditions. We know the
experience as the inner 'voice of conscience'. It is more difficult to describe or to exercise as a judgement-forming process. It is deeply related to the world and also deeply
individual. Deeper levels are called up in the *situation*, which
may come from established convictions out of past influences
or out of karmic origins.

The attitude or motive with which we are doing things is
always basically moral for it shapes the world in whatever
way we do it. It would be our task to teach in a way that
moral forces become a reality, not preaching 'shoulds' or
wishing for ideals or imposing principles. Moral would thus
mean discerning what is obvious and right for the human
future.

The following is an example of an exercise to practise the
research attitude in dealing with phenomena of modern life—
important for us in our media-bombarded world. This exercise can accompany Manichaean exercises for transformation. It works with observing an image from a newspaper or
magazine, or from TV advertising. (The 'make-believe'
advertising world might not be so happy with this exercise, as
it may expose hidden manipulations.) This is done in a group
of four or five people. Be aware that there is no right or wrong

judgement in what is found. We can learn from each individual viewpoint, and how the process functions in us.

1. Cognitive judgement:
   a) First reactions. The group receives an image, face down. Uncover image for 5 seconds and observe. Cover again. Share your first reaction in the group, in a short sentence or three words.
   b) Observing phenomenon. Reintroduce the image and observe closely, its composition, elements used, etc.
   Share observations in the group.
2. Aesthetic judgement:
   a) What values, impressions and qualities in the image touch you?
   b) What feelings come out of the image? What am I bringing to it out of myself?
   Share in group.
   Take a moment to bring self into balance. Centre self between inner and outer processes.
3. Moral judgement:
   a) Message of the whole. What do you understand as the message in this image? How is the image composed to give this message?
   b) What forces or beings could be working behind this phenomenon? What aim or moral will is in it? Who does it want to reach?
   c) What are the consequences for you out of encountering this? What moral will could you now take into the world, in your attentiveness, or lifestyle, or deeds? What do you take on, or let go of?
   Share what you wish to say in group. Where has the process touched you?

**Summary**
The I or spirit-ego in us is the force out of which we can choose to make the shift from passive to active. It is the spirit-ego that can observe itself as if from outside, that can hold the open space between observation and perceiving, that can oversee how our instrument functions, and can observe its

own activity. Thus every step of progress is on the way to becoming centred out of your own inner spirit source, finding your own true being. Out of the strength of this, one can then be selfless in observing and independent in discernment— objective, unconditional, non-judgemental as a social quality. You are fully present, and available for reality to speak to you, and to know its meaning.

## Judgement processes over the threshold
The foregoing schooling processes are necessary preparation for the independent individual approaching spiritual consciousness. First the soul forces are strengthened. We now consider indications for a threefold *integration of thinking, feeling and willing*, to deal with judgement-forming for the other side of the threshold.

### 1. *Thinking*
When we take what we see, or think we see, and want to look behind the sense perceptions, at first all is dark; we have no senses for this. The deep will urge to know and understand moves us on. If we are strong enough to face not knowing, to face nothingness, we let the lifeless dead thoughts flow into the void. The dead physical world thoughts are not useful to the other world. Then there may arise a new kind of activity, a creative thinking that resonates with the cosmic thought world.

### 2. *Feeling*
When we look inwards into the feeling life of our soul, we live in a weaving movement of dreamy experiences. Out of longing and deep passions, wanting to live life to the full, we are caught in our personal experiences. Now we must come to peace and stillness of heart, and let go of our subjective human passions. As these are overcome, we can experience a new kind of feeling, for what it means to be a human, to be part of humanity. A new power of life fills the soul, coming from cosmic sources.

### 3. *Willing*
When we look deeper into the self to the will forces that work

through our body, our consciousness is as if asleep—we cannot see how it functions. From our conscious thought sphere we can look down, shining our light into what is there, observing what is driving us. Then there may arise an intuitive knowing in the will. The relationship of thinking to the creative forces shows miracles—we know what to do, why, and when, filled with understanding in the same moment. You speak and act in harmony with the World All and with karmic consequences.

Ultimately we will manifest another kind of human 'beingness', standing in the world with a different gesture. Change in the world begins with change within oneself, within the human being.

# 7. Thresholds of Consciousness

**The worldwide crisis of humanity and the personal inner crisis in every human being**

*This chapter has been put together from notes of lectures given by Coenraad van Houten*

## The contemporary scene

All evidence is showing us that our consciousness is changing. Observe what is happening around you and in you. For instance:

Often impressions come into our consciousness that do not lend themselves to psychological interpretation or any other rational explanation.

Many books are appearing on the market describing an awakening new consciousness or awareness, or presence, indicating also that we may choose how we will live for a sustainable future globally, or a deeper meaning inwardly. We are enabled to participate in the challenges of our world, as never before in history!

Life also presents us with personal challenges and trials. Nearly everyone seems to be in a crisis situation, either outward or inner. We can identify either with our suffering or with the crisis as an opportunity for development. One way or another, we are all in a process of development. Contemporary conditions offer a moment of opportunity to find the spirit within.

We can call this an expansion of consciousness, crossing thresholds to other realms, from sense world to spiritual world. We belong to these *two* worlds. Ever more what belongs to one world works into the other—spirit into earthly, earthly into spiritual. The changes affect us personally, also in relations with others, and in experiences in life. Many soul phenomena of people today cannot be understood without this perspective. Each new generation seems to be more open to this. Therefore we need a new psychology to understand these threshold conditions and what happens as we approach the threshold between the two worlds. You may recognize some of these examples in yourself or in your environment:

**First example**
A central phenomenon of the approach to the threshold is what happens to our thinking, feeling and willing forces: they begin to separate, to function autonomously. They may speak with different inner voices and you do not know which is the true voice to listen to.

In thinking, one is caught up in the nerve-sense system, arguing every stimulus, or obsessed with knowledge, or caught in a particular model. One can imagine the most grandiose plans, but they do not fit reality. One can carry lofty ideals, philosophies, or 'shoulds', which we tell the world about but do not know how to put them into practice.

In feeling, an autism would be living so much in your own feelings you believe they are the truth; they take on a kind of autonomy, not aware you are stuck there. It works like an instinct—such as 'I love everybody'. We are sure we know the best way, but are not aware how we came to our value system.

In willing autism, you are ruled by unconscious drives. You have to move but are not conscious why you do it. Or you badly want to, but are lamed and cannot. The will is overtaken by trivialities of life and survival.

You may think one way, feel another and act in a different way. The ego has to now become active to harmonize and hold together the three which were formerly held together by the bodily organism but, since we are becoming free of bondage to the physical body, they become loose or confused.

**Second example**
There are two polar tendencies that play on us as we are approaching the threshold of consciousness. We can see them as archetypal of how polarities work, and also how we can benefit from this.

The one side gives us a sense of self and independence. It can give us an ego-inflation, an overestimation of self. We tend to be addicted to criticism of others, making others smaller to save our own being, criticizing the outer world for its imperfections. We deny having problems and deny our own inner islands. And of course we cannot accept any suggestion that our 'balloon of self' could be a false self-image. This side would hold to any sect, ritual or ideology that reinforces this tendency. The highest spirituality is the aim, and we are almost there! Or as in fanatic tendencies, our ideal deeds will be glorified in heaven.

The other side gives us a practical ability to live in the world. It gives the opposite message on the negative side, of underestimation of self. You are made to feel guilty, failed, incapable, not good enough, and are weighed down by a burden of past faults and how bad you have been. If you check whether you are really guilty, quite likely it is not true— just a waste of emotional energy. This force would keep us earthbound, not aspiring to anything spiritual; measurable facts constitute the only reality. It is too scary to even try to develop yourself... Safer to stay with a model or system. Or we are presented with dogmas, 'good teachers do not make mistakes', or 'it is not allowed to show weakness'. The outer world assails us with a high intelligence and logic that is actually dead. The fanatical tendency is to violence or destruction, to anti-life.

We need both these tendencies to develop a strong ego centre in uprightness, to move between and be creative. In today's world the two are working hand in hand, testing us by squeezing out any possibility for a middle, heart-filled human world. Both fill us with feelings of fear or of shame, which are signs of being on a threshold point, on the edge of developing something new.

### Third example
In my inner world are 'islands' which are closed off to consciousness (in extreme cases as problems of psychosis, neurosis, hysteria, etc.). The task is to bring them to con-

sciousness and transform them in a healthy way—such as in *learning from your destiny*. The educator should understand this, and neither force it nor try to be a healer. What helps is to make conscious and learn from, not 'live out'. There are many techniques that actually do not help this. For instance in America T groups had a method that pulled up such 'islands' out of the unconscious, but in a way that called up aggressive forces. One tendency is to stay in 'a good space' and ignore islands in the self. When we ignore them, however, they may work on another level and affect soul moods, as in depressions etc. Or you may see the same in other people and are not aware it is something of yourself—not aware it is your own island tendency. This leads to blaming the outer world, or denying that I have something to do with what comes to me. In this sense our environment is like a mirror. What lives in me plays itself out in the world around me. Hence we must always ask ourselves 'Has this phenomenon to do with me or not?'

There are many other characteristic threshold phenomena that could be cited. The process is accelerating with every generation. We live in a world where all is spiralling, in a vortex of forces of good and evil. We live as if in a house of mirrors—what is outside is a reflection of what lives inside. As a counterbalance, we could see every person as in a development process, and also see every person as on the threshold, struggling with it as we ourselves are, each in our own way. Karma is ever more actual. Our task is to see it, transform and understand it, and thereby change our way of being. We meet a destiny which tries to balance out our one-sidedness, to develop faculties we don't yet have.

We stand at a crucial time in a battle for the human soul, in the spirit of our time. There is not only negative material in us as consequences of the past, but also our goodness and potential. A way forward is to work with polarities, to find the open encounter space in between. Both sides will change because of the consciousness you bring into it.

## Basic threshold principles

We will describe briefly three thresholds, all of which really require much further elaboration and could be the subject of another book. Here we indicate what the educator needs to be aware of as basic principles, particularly as it concerns the process of spiritual research. Participants come with experiences, problems and questions of this nature.

These three thresholds are:

birth and death
day and night
inner and outer worlds.

### Birth and death

As this threshold opens, influences from before birth shine into life. Children ask questions. Impulses from pre-birth work into daily life. Before 1900 'pre-birth' was not a conscious question. Influences from 'afterlife' come to consciousness. In older years often questions come: 'What happens after this life.' Or in mid-life crisis questions come: 'Where have I come from? What is my task here?' Today, a longing for purpose is an urgent question. When one cannot hear it, depressions ensue, even suicide. This birth/death threshold has much to do with karma and reincarnation, and a question about the continuity of life.

For example, one can be born with longings or anxieties for what lies beyond this world. One can have memories of the past working on even into the constitution. Influences from friends who have died interpenetrate and enter our consciousness. Much literature is available on the threshold of death from those almost dying but returning to life. One knows 'there must be more to live for'.

These phenomena are not only to do with the beginning and end of life, but also within life—when we reach a 'dead-end', for instance, in our work or life situation, or in the artistic process when the artist reaches a nothing point. In designing exercises one also meets a nil point before the breakthrough of something new. In being creative there are many experiences of nothingness or of something new coming to life.

We meet these today as existential questions—to be or not to be? Death can threaten anywhere, and the question of what *is* 'life' is something we can no longer take for granted. Meeting this confrontation with an understanding of reincarnation and karma can give a basis for hope when all seems hopeless or pointless.

**Day and night**
The day works into the night, and night into day. This threshold has more to do with one's constitution, going to sleep and waking up. It is different for each person. For instance, sleep can be affected by esoteric work or activities engaged with during the day. It is becoming difficult for many people who are unable to sleep to wake up and hold their day consciousness. Sleeping pills are big business! The constitution may tend to be nerve-sense bound and so one cannot sleep; or one can be dreaming, half sleeping into nature, staying in a dreamy state, longing for another world.

It is a problem if we try to apply day logic to the night world. Rationality belongs to this side, drama of the dream to the other side. Dream pictures can be a confusion of elements or memories applied to the 'drama'; some dreams are messages of importance. We can learn to distinguish.

It is important to learn to hold the middle—of soul/spirit, soul/body—keeping a centre of balance so the human being finds a healthy rhythm between day and night. We are conscious enough to practise observing what we experience, and find the different qualities of these two crossings. The night world we carry in ourselves, in the soul, in feelings. The head tries to interpret; but beneath is the consequence of our activities. The problem is to distinguish pictures, interpretations, real feelings as 'sensing' a reality. The drama of threshold crossing produces new phenomena and new problems.

The day/night threshold is quite near for our consciousness

and can be schooled by learning exercises. For research purposes the day/night crossing is important, for what we do not see in the day is visible in the night—only we are not able to hold it as we wake up. In the night we are much more wise and see reality from its spiritual, moral side. The kind of activity we are engaged in during the day and how we fill that activity will decide what kind of invisible learning will happen in the night. We not only digest and evaluate our day, the higher worlds are also absorbing and digesting our thinking, speaking and doing, and are able to reinforce our faculties as a result. Through our conscious efforts in the day and pre- paring for the night, the breakthrough can often appear in the day, like a sudden insight out of nowhere. Often we can put a question to the night and receive a hint in the morning or next day, how to go further on the way. Or perhaps the question is wrong, and therefore the night does not answer! What is normally unconscious can come up into the feelings—feeling it is true or not, or feeling I must direct my will in another way.

### Inner and outer threshold

This refers to the inner threshold in the soul of conscious/ unconscious and the outer threshold of the boundary of the sense world. The inner threshold is beginning to open first. Psychologists last century saw certain phenomena but inter- preted wrongly what the unconscious really is. Freud was aware of new phenomena and searching for explanation. Jung found a collective unconscious and saw pictures but could not get further. He was clairvoyant, saw pictures, but could not come to an understanding of karma.

Goethe approached the outer threshold via sense obser- vation. He came to a boundary of an archetypal world, but knew if he beheld the phenomena well enough the truth would speak itself to him. He 'saw' the being of the tree. Goethe sought this way. He showed a way to the outer threshold.

In our inner world is a confusion of experiences. When we are not able to understand the inner, we see it outside the self in the world around and are not aware it is a mirror of one-self. Anxiety, fears, etc. can be a projection of the inner world put onto the outer. Conversely outer events may be a picture of what is happening within human souls. Many examples can be observed of such problems. For spiritual research, since we ourselves are the instrument, it is crucial to know how our instrument serves us—when am I experiencing my self and my own constitution and when am I in the reality of the other. In the physical world we can be corrected by the facts if we are mistaken. In the spiritual world our own moral sense must make the corrections or show us our mistakes.

Hence our development today goes through a struggle for what is true/untrue, real/unreal. It is today normal to have problems of soul—it is not pathological. To have old kinds of consciousness is pathological now. Today we feel anxiety for life, and anxiety for the self. It is remarkable that we can struggle consciously and question everything. This is part of the process to develop the strength and independence to hold oneself in the spiritual world as a being among beings, and to become a creative presence in both worlds.

## Historical context

'Only what we can be conscious of is real.' This is the modern human assumption. When earlier forms of spiritual con-sciousness were closed off, we turned to earthly experiences and interpretations as our only reality.

In history the outer threshold was the first to close—we lost the awareness of nature that had been normal for everyone. In old India, the outer world was regarded as maya. In older times the outer threshold was open; people could experience directly the nature beings. In about 3000 BC, Egyptian con-sciousness experienced 'what is above is also below': 'I don't think, the Gods think in me. The Pharaoh is my ego.' The Pharaoh was seen as the lowest being of the spiritual world. Then came a long process of gradually becoming aware 'I am a being in myself'. Philosophy starts to discuss human exis-tence. In Greek times Plato talked of a daemon inspiring us;

Aristotle saw a loss of spirituality coming and gave ten categories to save human truth; he gave a new logic. In the Middle Ages it was not allowed to be an independent spirit— we had to believe, follow, obey as the true religious path.

As the outer threshold closed, the inner world became more conscious. The outer became so solid, it reflected us back to ourselves. It has become like a mirror, helping us to become conscious and awake. Confronted! (Is the mirror me?) Now we receive outer sense perceptions, take in, must name, explain, interpret, find a concept, make our own mental images to hold. We play constantly with this process.

It was necessary to close the outer threshold so we could find individual certainty in earthly reality. As the old mysteries faded, their initiation methods became decadent. This has created consequences in the soul.

The more we can learn objectivity on the outer side, the more we can also develop the faculty to observe our inner world. When we look only with the 12 senses, however, we do not see the 'being' level. To school the senses means becoming less body-bound.

We learn to handle the inner world as if it is our outer world.

We school the inner world so we can perceive beyond surfaces of outer worlds and can understand what we perceive. We can develop our thinking/feeling/willing as transparent faculties.

Over the last 50 years many ways have been offered to satisfy the inner longing for the spiritual, some of which are not so healthy. If one encounters spiritual experiences, the questions must be asked: Could it be old clairvoyance? New clairvoyance? Schooled perception? Does it come from the outer or the inner threshold? Discernment of old or new should not worry us too much because the old faculties can be transformed to new faculties that are appropriate for our time and that are now possible.

New clairvoyance begins as a new understanding, not seeing visions or being a medium; we truly see what is there. The 12 senses give different touch points, windows to look through. We retain a sense-world awareness at the same time as being in the other world experience; we can control when and where to move, and know where we are. In fact we are often crossing inner and outer thresholds, but not aware that this is what is happening. Where actually is your threshold moment?!

As researcher the question is how to create a balance between inner and outer experiences, and also how to apply thinking, feeling and willing correctly, without our selfish ego being in the way.

## Categories of clairvoyance

We all have a bit of old clairvoyance. The past is after all our own history! As we begin to work on a new development, old faculties may also come up. In our unconscious, results of old clairvoyance from past times are there, resting in our constitution. Because we are crossing thresholds, a longing can awaken for what we once had. No one can judge for you, however, only you may decide what the experience means for you now.

1. *Atavistic seeing or hearing.* This is dependent on the physical constitution, i.e. is biologically based, and is usually linked with a slight disorder in the organism. Each organ of the body gives a particular kind of experience. Where an organ is weakened, an old faculty often appears. These experiences generally 'appear', as a vision or voice, sometimes in a reduced state of consciousness where the normally awake ego has given itself over to some other influence. It is evident that when these faculties are used today disorder of the organ can result; a further breakdown of the organism.

2. *Outer induced experiences.* As in 'getting high' by dancing, discotheque, drugs, medicines, opium, etc., the longing for experience is temporarily satisfied. It is also possible to work with imaginations presented in a way that directly affect the unconscious drives, avoiding the conscious middle, or in rituals to bring a special mood. It can also be done by an exercise that excarnates a person.

It is important for modern consciousness to have one's feet on the ground, maintain a healthy balance, and to be alert and observant while experiencing.

3. *Schooled clairvoyance.* Through inner exercises, meditation, transforming our thinking, feeling and willing for instance, a new level of understanding awakens. The knowing and understanding comes first; later come the visionary capacities, which Steiner called Imagination, Inspiration and Intuition. We can also experience 'knowing' as common sense, or sense for reality, or sense of truth.

The schooling path is never the same for all people. There are as many paths as individuals. Thus the task as an educator is to help find the right way for each person. Having a research attitude may change the nature of and reason for our inner path.

4. *New natural clairvoyance.* This is a new feeling-sensing for karma. Steiner predicted this would appear quite naturally, 'fairly soon'. Our experience has shown it to be real in our time. In destiny learning workshops, for instance, when a karmic truth is spoken, the person knows in their heart 'this is real'. The karma sense works in two directions: we may have a feeling-sense for the karmic past, or a feeling-sense for future consequences. We often meet people who have a 'natural' sense for reincarnation, for having lived before. We also meet people who are awakening to a 'humanity conscience' quality—what future we are creating by our deeds. We also individualize an inner conscience for our task. This new natural clairvoyance brings a fresh attitude in working with others as a fellow human being or as a possible maker of the destiny of another. We can no longer say, 'That is their problem, nothing to do with me.'

Many people have pictures that come out of the past, or sense an 'aura' around a person, not understanding what the experience is. Others may see nature with new eyes. Each has a particular opening, certain possibilities, and their own struggle on the threshold, according to their karmic past and future potential.

As we are crossing thresholds of consciousness, the karma force-field is the closest to daily life experience. We live in the earthly and spiritual force-fields. Karma touches us on all these thresholds. On crossing the outer threshold we enter the etheric world of nature; on the inner crossing we meet our soul in its journey of karma and development.

Many people have a mixture of the above. When going on a schooling path, we can overcome the old clairvoyance, it fades away, but comes back in new conscious faculties.

As spiritual researchers we are approaching thresholds, sometimes crossing over, bringing back something new, which is only creative when it can be realized in this world and can make a real contribution.

# 8. Human Encounter as a Prelude to Creative Spiritual Research

All that has been said in Part One of this book shows a new, creative way of encounter between the human being and his environment, beginning with a special question. A moment of 'breakthrough' at the threshold comes as a direct conscious encounter with the being or beingness of the spiritual sources behind the question. In older spiritual disciplines or forms of clairvoyance, this came as a divine revelation or vision, sometimes in a trance state. This has now changed. Each individual researcher has an encounter with the world of 'beings'. The meaning of what is perceived may be immediately obvious, or may only be realized some time later. The experience however is very real and very unusual—life changing!

But human encounter takes on another dimension as a threshold experience. We not only encounter one another as human beings. The same happens in every kind of encountering process between self and world. What *is* a real personal encounter then, rather than just making contact?

We use our 12 senses constantly to make contact with the outer world. We can also look inwards and observe our inner world. Our inner world meets the outer, the outer streams into our inner world. Is this an instinctive process, like animal instincts? Or is it a conscious engaging process, being aware what really happens? Or is it just reacting? The issue is how we are present and managing the space between inner and outer, between self and 'otherness'.

If we look at the process of encountering a person, then it could be that human encounter shows a unique meeting with a being that is not the same as me. If that succeeds we would be both changed afterwards. So we could say that even the smallest encounter with another human being could produce something new—perhaps a change in both—and therefore is not only unique and creative but can also be the strongest wellspring of creativity!

Today true encounter between human beings seems to be more difficult the more we individualize. At the same time when we discover a successful way of encountering, the wellspring of creativity will increase. It will also be a strong support for those people who want to do creative spiritual research. Hence as a support to the first part of this book we will now add two basic exercises to enhance the faculty of encounter.

## Exercise: the open space

Encounters can only happen when there is an open space between my inner soul awareness and my observed outer environment. With this openness I can investigate; if only reacting there can be no investigating or real observing. The first exercise therefore is for all forms of encounter, for it is necessary to create an open space between my inner world and the outer world.

*Aim:* This is an archetypal exercise for creating consciously the open space between your inner and outer worlds and strengthening your inner balance.

With a lemniscate movement, as in diagram over, you *rhythmically* move your focus of consciousness into the inner world and then into the outer world, accompanied by an alternating left and right hand movement. It is important to pause at the turning point to change consciously from one sphere to the other.

The experience can be enhanced by closing one's eyes when moving to the inner world and opening them for the outer world, with a specific object to be observed.

Repeat the total exercise (with both hands) three times and observe what changes. (For instance you may perceive the life quality of the outer object and lighting up of an inner awareness.)

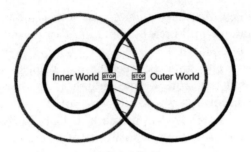

## Exercise: attitude preparation

*Aim:* To create the mood and presence for the encounter, ·creating an inner listening vessel to hold the open space.

As preparation for the actual encounter there are three ego activities.

1.  The first is learning to accept the other as he is, and also to accept yourself as you are. This means, for instance, seeing him as he is, even though he is not yet transformed, and the same for yourself. Accepting or saying 'yes' to how it is now requires an objective acknowledgement beyond sympathy and antipathy or standards of human quality.

2.  The second preparation for encounter is learning a selfless observation to see what is living in the other in their being, their struggles, the sense of their life. When I can live into the other with empathy I also experience him within myself. On a deeper level of recognizing the other for research, I look to the meaning of existence for the other and for myself. Can I perceive openly, free from prejudices, expectations and past experiences, with 'common sense' for what is real?

3.  The third preparation is to be fully awake, fully present and totally free of pretensions and of any underlying motives or wishes about what you would like to happen. This you can only do yourself, you cannot demand it of another. The moral side becomes evident: what is my real motivation for this encounter?

These attitudes are fundamentally a moral state of being. It is crucial to become these qualities, not just be able to use as a technique, or only understand as an intention. Thus the encounter for creative spiritual research has a special relation to the motivation level, for what, and why. Encounter must include awareness of *my own* morality.

Out of these three preparation qualities, the open space is held and the encounter may be realized.

There are many writings appearing today about spiritual encounters at the threshold and what this can mean. For example, from an experience of Otto Scharmer:

> At that moment, time slowed to complete stillness and I felt drawn in a direction above my physical body and began watching the whole scene from that other place. I felt my mind expanding to a moment of unparalleled clarity of awareness. I realized I was not the person I thought I was... I, my true Self, was still alive, more alive, more awake, more acutely present than ever before... At that moment, with everything gone, I suddenly felt released and free to encounter that other part of myself, the part that drew me into the future—into my future—and into a world that I might bring into reality with my life... Out of this profound opening of the heart, all my past commitments were released. I was about to discover what I would be doing in the next phase of my life.

He further explained this as 'presencing'.

> Presencing constitutes a third type of seeing, beyond seeing external reality and beyond even seeing from within the living whole. It is seeing from within the source from which the future whole is emerging, peering back at the present from the future. In these moments, we can feel linked to our highest future possibility and destiny. The source of intention shifts from our past to a future that depends on us...
>
> When this threshold is crossed collectively, people offer many different accounts of the experience. Some talk about extraordinary creativity, some about almost boundless energy, yet others about a dialogue where people forget who is saying what as the flow of discovery seems to gather

everyone together. Many simply say that what happens cannot be understood rationally because something that appears impossible has occurred—like a camel passing through the eye of the needle.*

In my book *Practising Destiny* seven ego activities are described for human encounter. In this book the encounter is connecting with the spiritual research learning path, which goes a step further and a deeper inner schooling is required. These seven ego activities are summarized in the following words:

Accept the other as he/she is, and accept yourself as you are
See the other as he/she is, and see yourself as you are
You appear as you are, being present and real
You create a counter-space, an open space
You act in the space, out of your present karmic possibilities
You experience something of the being of the other
You move rhythmically in and out of the encounter space

For the convenience of the reader, however, the seven activities as mentioned are given again below, in *Practising Destiny*, to give an indication of the encounter process.

### The seven ego activities for human encounter

1. Perceive and acknowledge the other person in the present moment with *full acceptance*, unconditionally, without prejudice or judgement or expectations. This acceptance, offering your being as a clear, undistorted mirror for the other, gives the strength to be who one is with open honesty.
2. Direct your attention to perceiving in a selfless way, using all 12 senses, observing the other person *with real interest* in his uniqueness. This requires withholding one's own reactions, irritations, associations, memories, sympathetic sentiments, etc., replacing subjective activity with an open empathy for how it is to be 'in his or her shoes'.

---

* See *Presence*, by Peter Senge, Otto Scharmer, Joseph Jaworski, Betty Sue Flowers, Doubleday, New York, ISBN 0-385-51624-x.

3. You are actively present in your most authentic self, discarding roles, pretence, reactions, protections, or superficial behaviour. Being fully there and 'real' also gives the other courage to be present in so far as he is able to in this moment—but this may not be demanded or expected. You can only be responsible for your own ego activity.

4. Ego activity now creates an *open space* between us. Interest and attention shifts from the other person to what can happen in the open space between us where both can appear. One must not dominate or want to fill the space, but be ready to give of oneself to serve whatever wants to come about. The best faculty for this is a feeling-sensing discernment of what lives in the moment and what it asks of you.

5. Having created the space, nothing further can happen unless we invest something of ourselves into the open space. This should be a creative free deed and requires some courage, when to act and when to hold back.

6. All the foregoing is preparation for the moment of *recognition* when you glimpse the true being of the other person. For instance, you may intuit why this person has to live within this karmic reality in this incarnation. Out of the recognition, destiny language may be spoken. Only by recognition by another can you know yourself, transform what hangs on from the past, or know the direction of your life intention. It is this recognition we all hope for.

7. A *breathing rhythmic movement* of encountering takes place, the ego actively offering itself to the other or withdrawing into itself. When this is honestly done, the encounter is held in balance and the reality of the present can be found. A healing, helping process can emerge.

\*　　\*　　\*

The encounter faculty is an urgent need in our times, in human relationships in all fields—work life, healing and therapy, social and marriage relationships, spiritual oriented groups or societies, etc. etc. It is also essential for the individual spiritual path where one will encounter outer and inner thresholds and new kinds of experiences.

# 9. The Becoming of the Mission of Mankind

The following is an exercise in four steps that schools our research faculties and our intuition to find creative answers for the needs of our time out of the forces of love and empathy. It opens the door to creative spiritual research in attitude and motivation, and supports an individual spiritual path.

## Step 1: Discovering our humanity and its aim. One mankind living under one sun

We begin with a leading image, a thinking activity that concentrates our awareness on the fact that we are the end result of all the incarnations we have gone through, from the Fall of Man until today. The destiny of the whole of mankind is in us. We realize that the destiny of our fellow beings has also been part of this whole process, continuously. We are one humanity, one creation, even though diversified in groups—such as races, nations, religions, 'chosen people', communities, radical groups, etc. etc. In our time, however, each person strives to become more and more individualized and independent.

The awareness of how the forces of destiny involve us continuously is deeply connected with the development of mankind, from the beginning of reincarnations until today. We come to an overview of the past history and future of mankind. This can lead to the awareness that we have been involved in many, many ways in the destiny of our fellow beings, ultimately including the whole evolution of mankind.

While pondering the general picture of humanity, I also become more aware of who I really am. Why, what for and for what reason do I have this destiny? What is the sense of it all? The thought that I have always been part of the destiny of all my fellow beings through many incarnations has a consequence in the understanding of my own destiny. The thought changes the meaning of my own destiny. The question why and for what do I live in this world is not answerable unless I understand, with this new longer perspective, that I was involved in all that has happened in our past history.

If we start to experience this thought, it can become rather disturbing. As soon as I try to understand what is happening today with the destiny of mankind, I wonder what part I have had—positive and helping or destroying and damaging, or anything in between. The deeper this thought enters me as a reality, so will this lead to the next stage which involves my deepest feelings towards my fellow beings. I am connected with them in any way imaginable, but a connection there is.

This leads to the next step, when I have the courage to observe my feeling life.

## Step 2: Compassion for the suffering of human beings and our karma together. The awareness of the deep crisis between our past and our possible future. Soul suffering

If the foregoing leading image is practised strongly enough, a consciousness arises of the suffering of humanity. Sensing this in our feeling life—not as a main thought now but an existential feeling—can lead to extreme crises of the human soul. We are connected with both the positive and negative events of history. In so far as we sense our connection with the destiny of all our fellow beings, many feelings can arise: those of despair, sadness, hopelessness, illusions, failures, guilt feelings, rebellion, exaggerated feeling of nobleness or being a chosen one—these are battling in many souls today. Many people try to cover up such deep feelings, as they can be unbearable. We have a past karma with much needing to be redeemed, and we know there is a future to come.

The suffering of humanity presents the question: What is or was my part in the destiny of the whole of mankind? This painful process, carried through with as much courage as possible, can become a deep sense of compassion, even culminating in a strong social impulse or an objective sensing-feeling compassion. It is not just an emotion but an existential experience. We become one with it; we carry the pain in our heart, or solar plexus. In the deepest form of original Buddhism this compassion for humanity was a major force. It seems as if today in many people this second stage takes on an inner, individual reality along with a concern for humanity on a global dimension. Actually it is a pain, but *a pain that transforms our feeling life to a sensing organ.* We are able to accept that suffering can be a necessity for development.

This now can lead to an objective feeling, of being involved and united with the destiny of all our fellow beings. One can discover, especially in every new generation, that people are beginning to sense this second phase in many different ways, but stronger and stronger. It has a future. It is an objective suffering of being involved, which does not need to be only personal suffering. A new social impulse clearly has to be born, and new ways have to be found. The stronger this objective suffering feeling becomes, the more it prepares for the next step, which involves our will. Perhaps we owe something to others, or have a need to atone for the past, or have something to thank others for.

Sadly two extremes can happen to this impulse, such as when a desire emerges to see oneself as a member of 'the chosen people', with the mission to lead mankind according to selected basic principles as the only solution for humanity. Or for the non-believers the only solution may be revolution, war or destruction.

## Step 3: Igniting the will to act

A very crucial transition arises between this suffering of our souls and a new will to transform our suffering into a will to act in healing. One can no longer say, 'It has nothing to do with me.' The future asks for a new social will. Within us is a slumbering will force to connect and act towards our fellow beings in a new way, a drive to improve the state of our existence.

This new force—which should not be confused with sympathy, or the need to love or be loved, and all the ways we know love so far—is one that leads to a new will to act. We struggle with the decision, in any moment, to act or not to act. In both cases we are nevertheless involved. This will is bound to our abilities and our bond to the past. Therefore the personal destiny comes back: What is my task? What can and should I do? What does my karma allow at this time? Is it the right time? The self-confrontation opens the way to realizing my deeper motivation, and the question how to go on from here. A deeper will may come up, realizing I have to act; I cannot do otherwise.

The consequences of my present deeds will create a new future. This is a new moral quality, to perceive the consequences of our deeds for our fellow beings, a *new faculty of awareness for consequences*. This will, born out of a new kind of interest and concern for humanity, has the quality of choice, of acting or not acting—it is open. We see the situation differently, because of our own inner changes.

It is free of any sentimentality or personal need; rather it has a need that comes out of understanding the sense and the mission of our time, which now asks for free deeds to answer the fundamental forces that are working today on a global scale. A free will begins to emerge as a possibility, creating a new future.

It is amazing how many people feel involved, for instance in parts of humanity where they have outwardly not been involved at all but feel connected, and sometimes even guilty of not having done anything. When anything is done through the compulsion of a certain group already it is spoiled. As we witness strong forces of self-love and own connections and special solutions on the one hand, we can also feel objective, acting for every fellow being that we are connected with in a way that they, consciously or unconsciously, are asking for.

## Step 4: A new birth of an objective love force. Perceiving the destiny forces working in the way we speak, act and create ourselves

At its peak the fourth step can lead to *a new kind of love force that does not make blind but makes visible* what the present struggle of mankind really is. It is a love that allows the forces of a future becoming to enter our present consciousness. This is a new way of perceiving, born out of the three former steps together. We are able to carry another, and can ask 'What ails thee?' with a deeper meaning to the question. Destiny has led you to this point. You are motivated out of recognizing a fellow being and what he is going through in his destiny. Out of this perception it may be obvious what now needs to be done.

Therefore this new love force has to be so strong that it allows something to come into my consciousness that I have never been aware of before. Millions of people want to help others but assume they can only help if the other meets their own expectations about the way of healing or helping.

This fourth step must transform the three steps together into a new kind of love, which creates a new kind of perceiving through the other's words—not as their content but as a way of speaking, moving and gesturing through which their real individuality tries to show itself.

In a karmic conversation, we need a strong acceptance and love force to stand it; selfishness has to go. Out of listening and identifying with the other's destiny composition the moral technique emerges for what has to be said at this moment, and in what way so it can be heard, and out of understanding what in a hidden way the other is waiting for. When this does happen, even in a small way, the other acknowledges it because he feels really understood. *This is a new force of social creativity.*

Each of these four steps has a consequence—an increase in consciousness and activity of the independent ego spirit. This spirit is awakening in you with each step, especially if you go into the feeling sphere via the karma forces. One could stop after step one, or after each step and not go further. Our feelings especially may thus far be bound to a social culture, or psychology, or personal concerns, or an ordinary reactive disposition. In the second step we move from our subjectivity to our feeling one with the whole of mankind. The new love brings a sacrificial quality which is also objective and general, and which makes the destiny events and the present task more and more visible.

The four steps create each other. The ego is given a way to bring together our thinking, feeling and willing, so that we evolve towards a new love force that radiates as a new kind of humanness. Without attaining to the objective love force, human evolution has no sense. With it we are able to participate in the process, freely taking on a creative activity and consequences.

*Clearly these four steps can also be seen as a path towards schooling the faculties that we need today to have a true encounter with another human being.*

*The 'karmic conversation' is the culmination of the destiny learning work, leading to a new quality of social life. This will transform the language of communication between people, to carry the truth of life in it. Thus communication will have a new meaning. Language will have a substance, instead of emptiness as is the modern trend. This is the great step towards an encounter conversation between two people, making it possible to hear and perceive in how their words are spoken what forces are battling in their souls. The great illusion that we are either very good or absolutely bad disappears rapidly, and the real question of who the other really is can become visible, audible to our karmic awareness.*

*Thus the exercise supports an individual spiritual path to develop greater awareness of karma forces, and builds a karmic ground for social relationships. The predicted new* 'natural clairvoyance' *is created, out of our own inner soul activity.*

# Further Reading

For readers who would like to study further the background of learning for spiritual research, we can recommend the following:

**Coenraad van Houten**
*Awakening the Will*
*Practising Destiny*
*The Threefold Nature of Destiny Learning*

**Bernard Lievegoed**
*Man on the Threshold*
*Battle for the Soul*

**Albert Soesman**
*The Twelve Senses*

**William Zeylmans van Emmichoven**
*The Foundation Stone*

**Emmanuel Zeylmans van Emmichoven**
Die Erkraftung des Herzens

**Peter Selg**
Michael und Christus
Rudolf Steiner und die Freie Hochschule fur Geistes Wissenschaft

**Rudolf Steiner**
*The Inner Nature of Man*
*The Riddle of Humanity*
*The Reappearance of Christ in the Etheric*
*How to Attain Knowledge of Higher Worlds*
*The Mission of the Archangel Michael*
*The World of the Senses and the World of the Spirit*
*The Laying of the Foundation Stone of the Anthroposophical Society*

First Class, School of Spiritual Science

And other contemporary writers, such as
**Otto Scharmer**
*Presence*
*Theory U*